SEVEN
FIGURE
SELLING

SEVEN FIGURE SELLING

DANIELLE KENNEDY

BERKLEY BOOKS, NEW YORK

SEVEN FIGURE SELLING

A Berkley Book / published by arrangement with
the author

PRINTING HISTORY
Berkley trade paperback edition / October 1996

The Putnam Berkley World Wide Web site address is
http://www.berkley.com/berkley

ISBN: 0-425-15302-9

BERKLEY®
Berkley Books are published by The Berkley Publishing Group,
200 Madison Avenue, New York, New York 10016.
BERKLEY and the "B" design
are trademarks belonging to Berkley Publishing Corporation.

10 9 8 7 6 5 4 3 2 1

THE WHO'S WHO OF
SEVEN FIGURE SELLING

GERT BOYLE, Columbia Sportswear

HELEN GURLEY BROWN, Editor, *Cosmopolitan*

BRENDA S. BURKE, Pecos River Learning Center

MARYLES CASTO, Casto Travel, Committee of 200

JENNY CRAIG, Jenny Craig International, Committee of 200

JOHN CREAN, Fleetwood Enterprises, Inc.

PETER AND KATHIE DAVIS, Founders, IDEA—The International Association for Fitness Professionals

ROBERT DAVIDSON, SPI, Inc., Los Angeles, California (Surface Protection Industries, Inc.)

DR. SHARON D'ORSIE, Eagle Environmental Health, Inc.

EVELYN ECHOLS, Echols International Travel and Hotel Training Schools, Committee of 200

LINDA FIELDS, Linda Fields Public Relations

EDIE FRASER, Public Affairs Group, Inc., Committee of 200

CAROLEE FRIEDLANDER, Carolee Designs, Inc., member and past president of the Committee of 200

JIM GAGAN, United Consumers Club

JOE GANDOLFO & ASSOCIATES, Ph.D., ChFC, CLU—Insurance

ALLAN GIBBY, CEO, Dynacom, Inc.

ELLEN GORDON, Tootsie Roll, Inc., Committee of 200

LOU HOLTZ, Head Football Coach, University of Notre Dame

TOM HOPKINS, Tom Hopkins International

BARRY KAYE, CLU, Barry Kaye Associates

DANIELLE KENNEDY, Danielle Kennedy Productions, Inc.

LIN LAM, Pacific Pioneer Insurance Co., Committee of 200

RICH LUISI, Electrolux Cleaning Systems

JIM MCMAHON, CTX Mortgage

JOHN MARCONI, Orange Coast Title Insurance Companies

ANGEL MARTINEZ, CEO, Rockport, Inc., a division of Reebok

JUDI SHEPPARD MISSETT, Jazzercise International, Committee of 200

JOSIE NATORI, Natori, Inc., Committee of 200

LANE NEMETH, Discovery Toys, Committee of 200

TONY PARINELLO, Tony Parinello and Associates

SHIRLEY PEPYS, NoJo, Inc., Committee of 200

JIM RHODE, SmartPractice, Inc.

JOY RIGGS, Employee Development Systems

KEN ROHL, Ken Rohl—KWC, Inc.

BLAKE RONEY, SANDIE TILLOTSON, STEVE LUND, AND NATHAN RICH, NuSkin International

FRED SEGAL, Fred Segal Stores

ROBERT SHOOK, best-selling author and salesman

DAVID STEITZ, Characters, Inc.

JACK SULLIVAN, Van Kasper & Company

JOEY TAMER, S.O.S., Inc.

HEIDA THURLOW, Chantal Cookware Corporation, Committee of 200

SOMERS WHITE, The Somers White Company, Phoenix, Arizona

*With Gratitude To JMJ
And Family*

CONTENTS

FOREWORD

"ANYONE WHOSE feet don't hurt, doesn't know what selling is." When Freddy Heineken, chairman of Heineken Breweries, uttered these words, he was remembering his humble sales beginnings when, as a kid, he peddled his father's beer from bar to bar to bar. But the "pain" in sales actually starts long before the selling. Before you can sell, you have to know how, because no matter what you may have heard, few folks are actually "born to sell."

The assumption that you have to be a born salesperson to succeed is only one of a number of misconceptions about sales success. Some think you have to be so consumed by the art of the deal, so single-minded in your pursuit, that everything else in life is secondary. It's not so.

Others think that reaching the top comes from mastering "surefire" techniques like preparing for sales presentations as if you were getting ready to launch World War III or repeating the prospect's name at least once a sentence. It doesn't.

Successful salespeople aren't necessarily glib talkers or smooth operators. They're not all driven by promises of untold wealth epitomized by fast cars, huge homes, and flashy jewelry. In fact *they* do not exist. Salespeople are individuals, each has a different hot button.

As the editor-in-chief of *Entrepreneur* magazine, the nation's small business authority, for nearly ten years, I have certainly read my share of articles and books promising to reveal the "one true way to achieve sales success." I've also met my share of experts who claimed to know the real secret to closing the deal. And on the whole, I've been left wanting. Wanting more information, more insights, more reality.

So when I assigned a writer to interview Danielle Kennedy, I wasn't honestly expecting a whole lot more than I'd read before. True, Kennedy was a sales professional of some renown, the author of five sales books, and a noted motivational speaker. Impressive credentials, but not necessarily unique. But in that interview Kennedy revealed something that was far from typical: She revealed herself.

Intrigued, I assigned Danielle to write a few sales articles. Pleased with what she wrote, I eventually asked her to contribute a monthly "Sales Success" column to *Entrepreneur*. Her first column impressed me even more because Kennedy showed she understood what I believe to be critical to success (sales or otherwise): Knowing sales tricks and techniques is not the secret; being comfortable with yourself is.

Still, none of this prepared me for meeting Danielle Kennedy. Only then did I understand what makes Danielle one of the planet's most successful salespeople, what enables her to achieve goals that millions merely aspire to. Danielle Kennedy does not sell with her head; her message comes from her heart and radiates from her soul.

Seven Figure Selling is not filled with tips, techniques, and strategies guaranteed to bring sales prowess. It is not a sales primer. It is more like a passport to the exalted world of sales superstars—the seven figure sellers. But Kennedy doesn't merely guide you through her world, she literally lets you in. It's as if you're the proverbial fly on the wall as Kennedy and her colleagues share, not their secrets, but their stories. And when you hear, in their own words, what makes these folks run, you'll learn how to adopt their wisdom as your own.

Danielle Kennedy takes you on a journey few ever experience. Be sure to pack plenty of passion and persistence, and, you too, may enter the world of seven figure sellers.

Rieva Lesonsky
Editor-in-Chief
Entrepreneur magazine

SEVEN
FIGURE
SELLING

INTRODUCTION

This is the fifth book I've written on sales, and it's dedicated to the salesperson who is restless and discontent. The one who just wants to get on with it. The one who is sick and tired of his or her roller-coaster sales career—a career riddled with anxiety over money and inconsistent sales performance. A somebody who is fed up with his or her own excuses, and ready to make a commitment to stretch into the top 2 percent—the highest paid and most respected in the field.

I knew I had to cover the externals of the process—the "what" of seven figure selling—because such achievement produces valuable and observable techniques worth imitating. However, I wanted to know more than just the "what." I wanted to know the "why." Why do legends become legends?

So I set out to find generous people who would be willing to tell me their stories. I wanted to hear juicy page-turner episodes from their lives that would give aspiring salespeople tons of hope, and a philosophy to live by that could dramatically move them in the direction they were previously unwilling to take.

Stories are great, but if they don't have a point, they waste the reader's time. So I turned into a Larry King. It didn't matter that I was talking to the most powerful legends in business, every interview started with the same instruction:

"Tell me stories about what you do and how you do it. How you got started, and what tough lessons you learned from hard-won experiences, including your mistakes. I need to hear stories that illustrate a point about specific techniques—techniques such as how you negotiate, or the best way you know how to pull yourself out of a slump."

I reminded them that readers remember good stories, and I was there to keep them on track because people's careers may end up depending on what they told me. It was seldom necessary to put my new seven figure pals back on track, as this book, which grew out of those interviews, proves.

I tape-recorded their interviews. My aim was to preserve the speaking voice of each person because I wanted this to be a book of voices—voices that the readers would hear long after they finished reading. Voices of endearing, generous teachers who continue to make their mark on our lives.

As time went on, *Seven Figure Selling* took on a life of its own, even selecting its own faculty of sales greats, while I went along for the ride. At first I wrote each page as an outsider looking in on the lives of legendary salespeople, but I knew I wasn't an outsider, so I added stories and lessons from my own seven figure history.

The teachers in this book come from every walk of life, with our own unique perspectives, proving that there are no special "types" that do better than others at sales.

William Zinsser says, "We write to learn," and I have learned more about myself, my peers, and the unique reasons each of us directed our own inner energies outward into the world of seven figure selling and entrepreneurship. We invite you to share in our hard-earned wisdom, and prosper.

DRIVEN WITH HUMAN ENERGY AND HEADED DUE NORTH

"When a salesman begins, he's a Nobody. He knocks on doors. He hands out business cards. He waits for people who never return his phone calls. He isn't sure he exists in the world."

—DAVID DORSEY, FROM *THE FORCE*

WHEN I FLEW to Boston to interview him, the first question I asked was how old he was when he made his first sale. What I was really fishing for was the source of his energy. Energy is what turns a nobody into a somebody. Sometimes it's born of discontent, or fear, or loneliness, or love of family, or a desire for financial security. It's an invisible, deep power and the driving force that takes people like Angel Martinez into the world of seven figure selling.

I heard about Angel when I was on the board of directors of the American Council on Exercise. At the age of thirty-nine, he already had a long selling history and was the current president of fitness for Reebok.

Martinez told me he started selling candy bars when he was nine years old. He sold them on the Bronx subways in the middle of winter to help bring food money in for the family. He had to work fast because people moved in and out of the trains in split seconds.

Both selling and later running channeled his discontent. He broke records in cross-country in high school and college. After he graduated, he started selling athletic shoes and soon saved enough money to open his own small shoe store in the San Francisco Bay area.

"I was more interested in building a business, than in making the next sale," said Martinez.

"I woke up each morning and set my mental compass to north for the day. North to me meant only one thing—converting as many people as possible who crossed my path in the next eight hours to a healthier lifestyle."

Then at the end of the day he asked himself a question:

"How did my passion translate into dollars today?"

His business plan is the compass he uses—merely an articulation of where north is. North is the direction of the markets he plans to penetrate. He reminds himself continually where north is, and he tries to take the most efficient approach to his goals each hour.

Not a list maker, but a picture taker, Angel keeps a clear snapshot in his mind of the best new ways to convert more prospects. If he intends to stay on target, he knows delegating is critical, so he takes pains to hire people who want to travel north with him.

"Each day I will only act on those things that take me north—the activities I am best at and most qualified to do. Over time I have learned where my mastery lies, and I rarely lose that focus."

Neither does insurance legend Joe Gandolfo. He started heading north at age twenty-two when he door-knocked at Louisiana State University selling life insurance. His first client, defensive right end on the LSU football team, died of cancer one year after Joe sold him life insurance.

"His wife wrote me a letter thanking me for selling her husband the policy. She was pregnant with their first child when he died."

Early in his career, perhaps, Gandolfo's own loneliness fueled his journey north. His mother died of cancer when he was twelve and his dad died when he was seventeen. Gandolfo grew up alone in a military school.

"Just me and God. And He's had His hand on me ever since."

Gandolfo wakes up every morning by 4:00 A.M. and attends Catholic Mass before going to work, which he refers to as his "vocation."

"Most people sleep too much. When they are up, they confuse motion with progress. I don't associate with anything except my family and my vocation. I don't socialize, and I don't waste time."

NEVER SAY DIE

There are dozens of never-say-diehards like Angel and Joe that we'll meet on the journey north. Introducing Committee of 200 member Evelyn Echols—a woman whose energy defies her age, a true silver fox and mischief maker. I got to soak up all her joy and wit over lunch one fall afternoon in downtown Chicago, my hometown. When the meal was over, I kept postponing our good-byes, unwilling to put an end to her recollection of wisdom-filled sales stories.

CEO of Echols International Travel and Hotel Training Schools, Evelyn translated her passion into big-time money by not letting any one person or isolated situation get the best of her. Before she founded the Travel and Hotel Institute, she earned her street smarts as a travel agent.

"I opened my own agency and the first year was really tough. I had this one painfully testy client. I bent over backwards for him, no matter how small the request, and it paid off in spades.

"One day I got a call from Mr. Toughie saying, 'You know, kid, if you could land that Pepsi account, you could become a legend in no time in the travel business. Here's a hot tip for you: The president of Pepsi, Al Steele, and star Joan Crawford are getting married and they have been put on a waiting list for the honeymoon suite on U.S. Cruise Lines. Get them that suite and Al Steele will crown you queen of the May.' "

Echols marched down to the cruise line and asked why Joan Crawford was on a waiting list. She was told that celebrities didn't get special deals. The cruise was booked solid and unless a cancellation came in, the Steeles were out of luck.

"So every day I went down to the cruise line and helped the staff open the mail looking for cancellations. Finally a cancellation came through but it was a lower-end suite. I knew there was no way Joan Crawford would take it, but by then I had taken the liberty of writing down the names and phone numbers of all the people who had first-class suites booked."

One man with a confirmed reservation lived in Wyoming. Forgetting there was a three-hour time difference, Evelyn picked up the phone and dialed. She woke the man out of a sound sleep.

"Don't ask me where I got the guts to say this: 'Sir, I just want you to know that you are standing in the way of my whole career.'

"He asked me how that could be, and I told him he had suite number U9092 on the U.S. Cruise Line and that I needed it desperately and would make him a deal. I had a suite that was not one-tenth as good as what he had booked, but if he would be willing to make an exchange with me, I would pay for his suite."

Echols was flat broke but was prepared to go to the bank to borrow the money. She knew it was a long shot and was flabbergasted when he told her he didn't really care what suite he had, then added, "God bless you. You can have it."

Evelyn called Al Steele and introduced herself. She told

him what had transpired but he didn't believe her. He said everyone at Pepsi and Joan's studio was working on booking them on the ship, but had been told it was impossible. Evelyn suggested he call U.S. Lines himself to confirm what she had done.

Of course it was true, and Steele had found his new miracle worker. So he dictated a memo to his secretary that said, "Evelyn Echols has the Pepsi-Cola account worldwide."

Evelyn still has a copy of the letter in her desk.

After the Echols interview I went back to my hotel and found a message from a friend in Houston. She gave me a lead about another Committee of 200 member, German-born Heida Thurlow. Heida, an engineer, turned saleswoman, turned entrepreneur, was the founder of Chantal Cookware Corporation. It was amazing how the kind of teachers I had hoped to find for this book were miraculously appearing out of nowhere.

In the first fifteen seconds I talked to Thurlow, I knew she had plenty of NSD (Never Say Die).

"I arrived in the U.S. in 1970. No one would hire me as an engineer—that's what my degree was in. Employers were put off because I was a single mother with two small children."

Out of necessity comes invention.

"I loved to cook and I was very frustrated because I couldn't find cookware that was both beautiful and functional. I thought, Aha! There's a need in the market I could fill."

Thurlow started combing department stores and specialty shops looking for other cookware product ideas. She found few U.S. stores that carried enamel-on-steel cookware, which was popular in Germany. She contacted the German Chamber of Commerce in Houston for a list of suppliers of enamel-on-steel pots and wrote to each asking for samples. She cooked in each of them and then selected the best.

Her parents lent her a small amount of cash, and she borrowed $50,000 from a local bank. She credits that loan to a loan officer who believed in her project.

Heida was able to get her line of cookware on the shelves of little mom and pop stores, but the big department stores would not take a gamble with such a new product.

"Just when I got going, I ran out of cash. It took me a long time to get another bank loan, so I sold my excess inventory over the weekends at flea markets. This gave me the necessary cash to keep Chantal going."

In the beginning Heida focused on unusual items such as the oval roasting pans she sold to Neiman Marcus. As she added more conventional frying pans and stock pots, she expanded marketing to other specialty stores, such as Crate & Barrel, Macy's, and Bloomingdales. By 1986 she was selling $3 million worth of Chantal cookware a year.

That was the year Heida discovered she had breast cancer.

"I got my chemotherapy on an outpatient basis. They gave me the medicine intravenously in my right hand; I learned to write with my left."

Today Thurlow's cancer is in remission, her $10 million company is thriving, and she holds thirteen patents of invention and design for cookware.

"My role model is my mother—she's a fighter, and she never took no for an answer. She always used to say, 'Where there's a will, there's a way.' I'm of that same spirit."

So is John Crean, a real never-say-die guy. I met Mr. Crean through Barbara Venezia, a close friend of mine and a sidekick of Crean on his cable television show "Home on the Range." John and Barbara teach their viewers how to cook up dishes in the kitchen John had built in his garage especially for the show. He does the show for fun and wants "He had fun" inscribed on his tombstone.

Crean, the CEO of Fleetwood Enterprises—manufacturers of recreational vehicles—started out selling window blinds.

"When I started out selling, there was a large window blind account which was contracted to another supplier because the sales rep and the owners were drinking buddies. Even though my price was lower, I couldn't get those owners to even look at what I had to offer. They would hardly give me the time of day, but every time I would go by their place I would call on them.

"One night I was coming back from my rounds of delivery. I was very tired and it was late, and the light was on in their office. That little voice inside of me said, 'Stop in.'

"Then I thought, Oh hell, why should I stop there? But then I figured, why not? So I walked in. One of the partners was pacing up and down and madder than a wet hen.

"He said to me, ' I want to look at your prices. How soon can you deliver?'

" 'Next week.' "

John was given the order for the following week's production on the spot.

"All I could do was repeat to him how great it was to get his business. Then I asked him why he changed his mind and decided to give me an order.

"He told me he should have been out of his office two hours ago. Instead he had been sitting and waiting for a venetian blind delivery for his trailers. The delivery never showed up. This kind of stuff had been happening for months and he was sick and tired of it."

FORGET ABOUT THE OUTCOME

What if John had quit following through?

What if the man had refused to give up his suite for Evelyn's client?

What if Al Steele had been insulted by Evelyn's aggressiveness?

What if Heida had given up when she ran out of money or found out she had breast cancer?

There is no room in the big time for "what ifs." Seven figure performers learn how to live with uncertainty. It is the factor I have been tested on most during my career.

A few years ago I wanted to take the art of speechmaking to a more exciting and motivating level. Because of my drama and dance background I dreamt of introducing some musical moments into my keynote speeches to bring the message home more dramatically than in the traditional ninety-minute lecture.

At first the dream was exciting, but after the honeymoon stage of my thinking subsided, I came down to earth and realized I was scared silly and that my idea might have been dumb. It was during one of my especially annoying "what if" days that fear began to get its way with me. My inner demons began whispering:

What if people laugh at you when you sing and dance?

What if people think you are trying to become the Liza Minnelli of motivational speaking?

What if you bomb?

Fear had taken over my body and spirit. It felt as if I had a body cast plastered on me from the inside out. I lost all perspective.

I tried giving myself a "mental enema"—a home remedy of mine I have been using for years. I sit in a chair, close my eyes, blank out my mind, and concentrate on one thing and one thing only—my breathing. I pretend there is a clear button on my forehead and push on it in order to clear out all the bad thoughts, and make way for concentrated, relaxed breathing.

Stress is created in the mind by my thoughts, and when I exercise mind control I can eliminate stress. Usually it works, but on that particular day I could not connect with my breathing or make peace with myself. I tried talking to family and friends who supported my dream, but I was frozen stiff inside. Then I asked myself a question: What are you afraid of, Danielle?

All I cared about was outcomes. I was looking for a guarantee that this program would be a big success. Faith-filled salespeople don't do this to themselves. I had let myself forget that. I was mentally heading south.

In the midst of rehearsing for my new keynote, I got an okay to interview Carolee Friedlander. Just in the nick of time I got to fly to Manhattan and be reminded by this tall, lean, clear-headed woman just how important living in the moment really is. As president/CEO of Carolee Designs, Inc., she heads one of the most successful fashion jewelry companies in the world.

She recalls: "In the early days of building my business I would have been doomed if I concentrated on outcomes. I schlepped my large, heavy bags of jewelry into buyers' offices and department stores for years. I worked on designs all night and spent all day in lines only to hear some sarcastic buyer say, 'Do you really think this is saleable?' "

The world forces us to look at outcomes. Is this saleable? Will you be successful? But top salespeople and entrepreneurs have one thing in common—rock-steady faith in what they are doing and the discipline to do it. Carolee would never allow herself to question outcomes and the chance of their success.

"I wake up with a certainty about my work every day. Without it, I might as well forget about my dreams and visions."

I got my second reminder about outcomes on a visit to Arizona from Businessman of the Year, Phoenix-based Jim Rhode, president of SmartPractice, a $30 million company that markets and distributes products to health care providers.

"A couple of years ago we hardly knew what scrubs [medical smocks] were, and now we sell a lot of them. In 1988 we sold no latex gloves and certainly no non-latex gloves. Today, they are an important part of our business. I have no idea how we will make our living in 1999."

Flying blind does not bother Jim. He doesn't have to know exactly what the outcomes are going to be for SmartPractice. Rhode was barely thirty years old when he began to follow his instincts and realized that dentists were going to have to start making strategic changes in the way they did business.

It was the early seventies and the birthrate had dropped substantially, resulting in fewer cavities to fill and less orthodontia repair work in the future.

So he and his wife Naomi (a dental hygienist at the time) began to educate dentists. He started teaching dentists basic follow-up sales skills such as writing thank-you notes and sending mail-outs with six-month checkup reminders.

"But the dentists needed a handy resource for the thank-you notes, so our company produced them. We had no idea ahead of time we were going to make them."

Today Rhode has a huge catalog of products for dentists, veterinarians, and other health care professionals.

"Thirty years ago I never would have guessed I'd be in this business today."

One woman who doesn't give a hoot about outcomes is Brenda S. Burke. Probably North America's leading saleswoman in the personal improvement and corporate training field, Burke did six million in sales last year for Pecos River Learning Center. Founders Larry and Elizabeth Wilson recruited Brenda in 1988 fresh out of the health care field.

"I was the volunteer director in a Phoenix hospital. My job was to help people with mental disorders and chemical dependencies make a smooth transition back into society. I did this by involving them in volunteer work. I never wanted to be in sales. My dad was an automobile salesman and dealer. He was a great one, but I didn't want any part of it. I didn't understand back then that the pros sell to serve.

"When my husband and I moved to Santa Fe, New Mexico, I heard about the wonderful things that were going on at Pecos. Larry and Elizabeth Wilson were making a difference in the lives of not only companies like DuPont, Kodak, and General Motors, but also Coach Lou Holtz and the coaching staff at Notre Dame. They were all going through Wilson's special training and his Changing the Game leadership course.

"Once I went through the program myself, including the

outdoors day, I knew I could deeply help people by recruiting them. This was not the conventional pump-'em-up-for-three-days-and-let-'em-go type seminar. This offered a curriculum that a person could use throughout a lifetime. It changed me, 'the skeptic,' so I knew firsthand what it could do for others.

"Never once have I thought about how much money I make or how many clients I recruit. I transferred my counseling skills to sales. I am doing the world a great service by making them aware of Pecos River Learning Center. Larry Wilson and our team really are 'changing the game.' "

Jim Rhode, Carolee Friedlander, and Brenda Burke remind us that when we quit worrying about outcomes and allow ourselves to be swept away in the work, success can, and oftentimes will, unexpectedly arrive at our door. It is helpful for us to remember that we all fly blind—to live each day without seeing or being guaranteed of specific outcomes.

A man of deep faith, Joe Gandolfo gives good advice for the worry-warts and outcome seekers:

"Go to bed. God's up all night anyway. Let him worry about it."

AWARE, WILLING, AND DETACHED

The late theologian Anthony DeMello said, "You are only a slave to what you are unaware of." There was no one more unaware of how to control my sales destiny than myself. I entered the sales force in 1972, six months pregnant with my fifth child and flat broke.

My first sales manager was a tough taskmaster whose only bit of advice was to "go door-knocking." I reminded her of how very pregnant I was, but in her book, pregnancies were a lousy excuse. Her favorite story was about an eighteen-year-old man from Los Angeles who, tired of carrying steel everyday, dreamt of becoming a great salesman. The only thing that stood between him and his dream was the fact that he didn't own a suit.

Unwilling to give up so soon, this resourceful young man decided to dig up his old high school band uniform and wear it when calling on prospects. The rest of his story is sales history. The kid in the band uniform became a legendary seven-figure salesman and later became the world-class sales trainer and author Tom Hopkins.

Other people's stories have always motivated me. I got all fired up after she told me about Hopkins, and I waddled out of the office eager to prospect. *Willingly* I headed north. Little did I know that being *willing* instead of *defiant* was all that was necessary to kick off a successful first year in sales.

That first year, I literally had no competition in the marketplace. The streets were deserted. I didn't realize how many defiant salespeople were back at the office waiting for telephones to ring, customers to fall into their laps, and leads to spring generously from the lips of management.

Each of us has a choice. We can choose to dwell on our negative messages. Negative thoughts exhaust us, and ultimately lead to our own recessionary sales conditions. Or we can stop thinking and take immediate, positive action. Salespeople think too much and take too little action.

Here's how I avoid sales slumps: Experience taught me that prospecting is the one activity that keeps me loaded with leads and flush with money, and my company in the black. Every time I stop prospecting, I fire myself; every time I start prospecting, I rehire myself.

Sometimes it's hard to keep prospecting when I get a good lead, because I get excited and am tempted to put all my eggs in one basket. I know from experience I cannot do that. I can't stop marketing as soon as I connect with a prospective customer. This leads me to become anxious and overly attached to the new customer, which ultimately discourages the customer from telling me the truth about his or her circumstances. The customer feels too pressured and obligated by me, and this pushes him or her away. The customer gets the impression that I am desperate to sell something. And the customer is right.

EASE ON DOWN THE ROAD

"Don't you carry nothing that might be a load," sang little Dorothy, eager to meet the great wizard. Wasn't I told once by some sales manager to stay heavy in debt in order to motivate myself to sell more? Didn't he say something like "The more debt you acquire, the more motivated you'll become to earn a six or seven figure income."

Most of us do not begin a sales career or a new business venture debt free. I wish I had been aware of that important lesson earlier in my journey north. Too often we think we are taking the easy way out, placing debt on top of debt, only to discover that our original problems have multiplied. Ultimately arriving at the big time with as little debt as possible allows us the privilege of stewarding our money. Stewards act responsibly by solely concerning themselves with their customers' needs, saving part of every commission check received, and giving away sometimes 50 percent of their income to the less fortunate.

During the early years of building his company, Jim Rhode refinanced his house and used all his savings to keep his business growing. But, he explains, "I couldn't wait to clear the debt because I learned as a kid that every bit you borrow you have to pay back."

Rhode explains that if borrowing becomes necessary and business is slow, keep in mind that "No vendor in the world will turn their back on you if you tell the truth. During one of our more challenging early years, we were sometimes sixty or ninety days late. I called everybody from my banker to my vendors and asked what method of payment we could work out.

"Too many times people get afraid and hide. Tell the truth and stay in touch. But the best advice in the world is to avoid borrowing if at all possible. I can honestly say having money has never motivated me, but not having money did."

A WORK IN PROGRESS

I met Allan Gibby when he was in his late twenties. He was a cameraman on a cable TV show I was hostessing in Orange County, California. Back then he was a young and devoted husband and father, and today he is Allan Gibby, Owner/President of the highly successful Dynacom team (producers of ESPN sports programming) and an even more devoted husband and father.

I felt like a proud big sister the day I got to interview this proven sales wiz and cutting-edge entrepreneur. Nothing had changed about Allan since our last visit together. Success hadn't tainted his pure spirit and deep devotion to his family and work ethic. I knew that Allan would have many valuable lessons to teach us.

"Every job I have ever had has prepared me for the next stage of my career. I've always said, 'This isn't forever, but just for now and a training ground for the future.'

"When I was twenty-one, I was laying steel in swimming pools in 110-degree weather. I remember thinking that the experience was teaching me what I did *not* want to do for the rest of my life."

The experiences Allan had as a young missionary in his church prepared him to make cold calls later on in his career, to customers thinking of buying airtime.

I passed on the Allan Gibby Work-in-Progress Method to one of my sons, now vice president of sales for a production company in Hollywood. After graduating from college, he was offered a job at one of the largest, most prestigious advertising agencies in Los Angeles. The pay was very low and the duties were servile. Unless my son looked closely, I feared he would mistake the job as being that of a glorified messenger boy.

"You mean you'll get to know people in every department of the company?" I asked him.

"Yeah, because I'll be the one sharpening their pencils," he said.

"Sounds like a work in progress," I said.

"Meaning?"

"Meaning the job has possibilities."

"Yes, but sharpening pencils?"

"If it's in the direction you're headed, become the best pencil sharpener they've ever hired and you'll stand out like a shining star."

Within six months, he knew every employee on a first name basis. He took me to lunch one day and showed me around like he owned the place. He was not only sharpening pencils, but also sharpening his ideas and submitting them to staff for ad campaigns.

He got to know one of the executives, who was also on the board of directors for the production company he works for now. This man became my son's friend and mentor and opened many doors in his future.

I got the same advice from Fred Segal, owner of Fred Segal Stores in Los Angeles.

"My entire life has been a huge training ground. I didn't know this when I was younger but every single step I've made in my career has prepared me for where I was going next. I started out thirty-five years ago as a manufacturer's representative for a medium-priced sportswear company. After a short while, I realized I had an inclination for fashion and began designing the line for the company without realizing that was what I was doing."

He got the idea for fashion blue-jeans when he was out making sales calls. Jeans were selling for only $2.99 in the 1950s. He thought about making jeans a fashion statement and selling them for $20 a pair. Making sales calls and being the man on the street gave him the knowledge of what the customer wanted. Without realizing it, this knowledge helped him prepare for his next big move north.

"After five years with that company, I proposed the idea of selling designer jeans, not in the basement of a store, but on the main level, and doing so for $20 a pair. My company didn't buy the idea so I left and started my own jean sportwear business in 1958.

"Steve McQueen saw a pair of my jeans and said he wanted to wear them while riding for the U.S. motorcycle team. Then a famous Hollywood hair designer bought them for all of his hairstylists.

"Stars like Cher, Bobby Darin, and Julie Andrews would come into the shop and want to know where his stylists got their jeans. The next thing I knew half of Hollywood was walking around in my jeans and being photographed in them as well. Then people started to line up around the block to buy my jeans."

It all started when he was a sales rep, a work in progress, wondering what life had in store for him.

BECOME COMFORTABLE WITH FEAR

To some degree, we all learned how to deal with fear.

Reebok's Angel Martinez put it this way.

"Every day I am afraid. But I accept its presence now. This acknowledgment of its presence is as far as it goes. Fear no longer controls me. When I was a cross-country runner in high school and college, there was always that time in the race when I decided that I was going to go for it, and it was time to break away from the pack. In that moment feelings of tremendous fear would rush through me.

"First I would freak out and think, I can't finish at this pace.

There was that self-preservation factor: God, I'm gonna die. But I also knew that if I backed off, I would lose. So I put my head down and went for it, one breath at a time, to see what would happen.

"If I were to have let myself think for one second and really consider all the possible outcomes, I would have lost. But instead, once I decided in my head to go for it, I would let my body do the work and the rest of me would follow along for the ride."

When I managed a sales team I encountered people who subconsciously stopped themselves short of greatness in order to go back to their comfort zone of mediocrity. One woman tripled her prospecting list and began logging in sales like she'd never done before; however, in midstream she did the opposite of what Angel suggests.

Instead of going for it in spite of her new feelings of fear, she set out to block her progress. She'd drop little hints to me and others:

"My husband hates it when I'm not home to make his dinner on time.

"All these additional clients are very demanding. What if I can't deliver what I promise?

"It doesn't matter if I make more money, we'll just get deeper into debt anyway."

Within six months she had dropped out of the business. She quit shortly after her best month in sales. It's almost as if she would not allow herself to go any further. The last time I saw her she had put on a lot of weight and was back working as a cocktail waitress. When I looked her straight in the eye, I saw resignation in her expression.

I felt sad when we parted and suddenly I knew why. Fear had gotten its way with her. When fear gets its way, the first thing to go is the joy that is present in the eyes of the passionate person in pursuit of a dream.

Brenda Burke's biggest fear in her cold calling days was contacting the presidents of organizations. This was her market;

the calls had to be made. There was no way of getting around it.

"The decision to hire our company must come from the top because it is not inexpensive, conventional training that we offer. I was deathly afraid to call on these 'giants of industry.' I was convinced there wasn't anything I could teach them or talk to them about that they didn't already know.

"Once I gathered up the strength to make the call, I realized they were all just like the rest of us. The title, power, or money did not make them less human. Pecos is a human resource place and we had solutions to human problems that resulted from the human condition. All I had to say was 'How can we help you and your team?' I was left amazed, humbled, and fearless by their answers."

Author Martin Whitney says, "Fearful people are usually obsessed about outcomes. When they find themselves putting forth efforts and fretting over whether their efforts will be compensated, or what the reactions will be to those efforts, they are expecting the receipt of acceptance in order to value their work. They turn their entire self-worth into the receiver's hands."

I learned that as I moved closer to north, fear tried to invade my being. Now that I am fifty-one years old, I don't give fear half the chances to invade my thoughts. I stop my own fearful thought process by either administering a mental enema or speaking a simple instruction to myself:

"Be still."

I keep repeating it in a whisper until the fear subsides. At those times I remember that I am like a child who needs the comforting arms of mother after a fall. I've been everybody else's mother, isn't it time to be my own?

When I work at the principal's office at my daughter's school, children are constantly coming in from the playground with everything from scraped knees and paper cuts, to head and stomach aches. Most of the complaints are highly exaggerated, but I always treat each upset with deep concern and a therapeutic story.

"Come over here and let me look at that knee." They get a clean-up, fresh Band-Aid, and a good story while sitting on my lap.

"I'm going to show you something. See this scar?" I say, pointing to my knee. "This scar is thirty years old. Flipped right over the handlebars going down a hill on my bike when I was twelve years old."

Kids and adults act exactly the same when they get afraid. Everyone responds beautifully to comforting and "me too" type stories that remind us that fear and failure can attach itself even to the best of us.

Angel's story of confronting fear on the running track has since motivated me to do the same at those fearful times in my own life when I needed to continue in spite of myself and my fear. We all need to share our battles with fear in hope that our own realizations and revelations in the face of fear can aid in alleviating another's similar struggle.

In my company I used to love holding sales meetings centering on failure. Others' failures give us all hope. I would ask my sales team these questions:

What did you learn from your last failing experience?

How can you put that lesson to practice in your life in order to get closer to the big time?

Other people's stories invigorate us and motivate us to press on. Recently, while I was lecturing in Philadelphia, a very tiny, handicapped woman in a wheelchair came up to me and told me a story that made my day.

"The first time I heard you on tape talk about how you went out prospecting with a big pregnant belly, I said to myself, 'If she can do it, so can I. Danielle had a baby in her belly to drag around and I have this wheelchair.' So off I went. Then I started giving speeches to other handicapped people like myself. I tell them it doesn't make a damn bit of difference to people how you serve them as long as you serve them.

"Wheelchairs, big bellies, you name it, people just want service. It's my mind and the commitment I'm willing to make that governs how fast and effective I can be for those I serve.

"Let's face it, Danielle. You were able to get sixteen times more things accomplished with a baby in your belly and four children underfoot than the average, unencumbered, lazy loaf who seems to be waiting for a break. Your example took away my fear and got my wheels spinning."

Now she's bringing a whole bunch of other wheels with her to the big time. This woman made a decision not to allow fear to block her journey. She said no to the demons inside of her who tried to insist that she stay put. These demons show up inside everyone.

One of my favorite fearless saleswomen is President of Discovery Toys Lane Nemeth. I delivered the keynote address to the Discovery Toy team back in 1986, and Lane and I became fast friends. She was one of the first names on my hit list for *Seven Figure Selling*.

She says, "When I feel fear come up inside of me through negative thoughts, I literally yell out loud 'Go Away. Stop. Get Out.' It's the death of an entrepreneur to make any decision based on fear.

"My sales manager came in recently and gave me a report showing profits slightly down for the month. Then he asked me about a project we had planned for March. Without realizing it, for about five minutes I allowed fear to speak for me; I told him to postpone the work. Then I stopped myself and told him to forget what I had just said and to keep moving forward. Never, ever let fear make decisions for you. Fight back."

CHOOSE YOUR TRAVEL COMPANIONS WISELY

The teachers in this book seek out the companionship and support of those who are not controlled by fear. I asked Lane

Nemeth how she knows when someone is free from fear. "They don't say or do negative things. And they will share their stories of failure with you because they know each story possesses a hidden jewel, a lesson that can take you to the top. They are just plain generous and aren't holding back out of envy."

I went to one of the most positive entrepreneurs I know— Judi Sheppard Missett, the beautiful dancer/choreographer and founder of Jazzercise International—and asked her about choosing the right people to grow with along the way.

"No one who is negative makes it for more than five minutes at Jazzercise because the place is full of happy people. Picture a sunny afternoon at the beach and a big, blue sky. Out of nowhere a big black cloud appears. It is so noticeable. The heat of the sun is missing. Next the rain breaks. You know what to do: grab your towel and go."

Nathaniel Brandon says, "Never marry someone who is not a friend of your excitement." This is a good piece of advice for those of us headed north. I have never traveled long with someone who was not a friend of my passion, my excitement, and my dreams.

Once I detect I have a fear-filled, negative soul on my hands, I politely step out of the way. If I find myself stuck in a conversation with that type of a person, I say I have a commitment to fulfill and then excuse myself. The word "commitment" carries a lot of weight and covers a multitude of sins, including excusing myself to go sit in a corner and talk to the most fascinating person I know at that particular moment— me.

It takes courage. Some people say they cannot get rid of negative people. Maybe the truth of the matter is we don't want to get rid of the negative people in our lives. Many people subconsciously crave and enjoy the negativity and gossip provided by negative people.

My friend Pat McCormack, a four-time Olympic gold medalist in high diving, arranged for me to have a telephone interview with Helen Gurley Brown. Helen turned her secretarial job into a seven figure magazine career. She is now the editor of *Cosmopolitan* magazine, with twenty-seven international editions. I found her to be loaded with wisdom, which will surface throughout the book. To avoid time-wasting people, she uses "cut-off maneuvers" to get rid of people who stay on the phone too long.

"One trick is not to take the phone call in the first place. Screen calls with an answering machine, voice mail, secretary, or just have the self-control to let the phone ring. But if you get trapped and find yourself trying to get free, just tell the time-waster you have people waiting and must leave now. I try to be polite and say it was good of them to phone in, but now I must go!"

Join the Optimists Along the Way

One of the finest self-help books written in the last fifty years is Martin Seligman's *Learned Optimism*. Every legend profiled in this book has mastered the techniques Seligman teaches. For the past thirty years he has researched students, salespeople, company presidents, and sports stars. His research proved over and over that people who are basically optimistic get to where they want to go.

In his book Seligman talks about a distinctive "explanatory style." He looked for it when the Metropolitan Insurance Company hired him to find out why the first-year turnover rate among their sales force was so high.

"Pessimistic salesmen will say permanent, pervasive things to themselves, like 'I'm no good' or 'No one wants to buy insurance from me,' or 'I can't even get to first base.'

"This will undoubtedly produce the giving-up response and make it harder to dial the next prospect. After several such episodes, I predicted, the pessimistic agent will quit for the evening—and eventually quit altogether."

Met Life's research turned out to be very valid and resulted in the company revamping their entire testing program for new hires. Career profile tests that attempted to identify potential for success based on talent alone were no longer a strong argument for hiring insurance agents. A test was added to the interview process that enabled management to discover up front how optimistic or pessimistic a particular candidate was. It was proven over and over again that talent combined with a pessimistic attitude did not necessarily produce a top producing agent.

In the past many optimists were eliminated in the hiring process because their career profile did not show a strong talent. It was discovered, however, that an optimist with even a minimal amount of talent could become a great insurance agent because of his or her ability to begin again over and over after facing rejection.

When people are optimistic, they are also trainable. What they lack in talent they make up for in willingness.

"I've always said I had more guts than talent," says Helen Gurley Brown. "I'm still taking risks and loving it. Last year I got this great idea for a vodka advertisement. I had the art department do some wonderful layouts, and I called up the head of this big vodka company and asked him if I could come out to his office and pitch my idea.

"The ad showed a woman in a sexy bathing suit on the beach with her lover. They were drinking vodka together, but she was also using the vodka to give him a rub down. I remembered when I was young having a marvelous time with a beau out in Malibu one afternoon. We were sipping vodka and giving each other back rubs with it at the same time.

"Well, the president of the vodka company was not impressed! He didn't throw me out of his office, but things got pretty tense. Until this day I still think it was a brilliant idea."

My friends Peter and Kathie Davis, the founders of IDEA—The International Association for Fitness Professionals—stayed optimistic after their bookkeeper made a substantial error.

"After Kathie and I calmed down, we decided to put on a new mid-year program—a personal training seminar—instead of waiting until summer, for our next annual conference.

"Our members were asking for it, and we felt maybe this error was the motivation to get us started. Four months later we had our mid-year program, which turned out to be another industry winner and recouped some of the money. The crisis was a great learning experience too. We had never been in a crisis before, so if another one comes up, we will know what to do."

Judi Sheppard Missett got Jazzercise off the ground shortly after she was fired from an elite spa.

"It was a few days before Christmas, my husband was out of work, and we had a little one at home. Up until then I was working at a well-known spa and doing my own thing through recreation departments. After I was fired, I went back to the recreation people and asked for all the rent time they would give me. That is when Jazzercise began to take off."

The optimist takes nothing personally, and moves on quickly to the next cold call or opportunity.

"Next" could be the most important word in the optimist's vocabulary.

USING IMAGINATION AS A POWERFUL BUSINESS FORCE

Carolee Friedlander's imagination began working overtime in her kitchen over twenty years ago when she used Oreo cookies as sample molds for jewelry casting.

"I was in my kitchen trying to figure out how to cast while

my two little toddlers crawled around on the floor. I was looking for something in the kitchen cabinet that I could use over and over again, a surface to test different types of waxes. I grabbed the tops of Oreo cookies to test them out in different ways and passed the bottoms on to my little ones crawling around the floor."

The few necklaces and bracelets she designed from Oreos have exploded into a multimillion-dollar fashion jewelry business. Here is one of many innovations her imagination has brought into that industry:

"Fashion jewelry used to be laid out flat in a glass case like cookies in a bakery, losing all its sculptural excitement and sparkle," she recalls.

"I believe that to heighten sales, store biz should be show biz. We lifted from the theatre by creating little stage sets within individual cases, utilizing height and depth as well as width, then vertically tiering the cases depending on their proportion. Then we provocatively themed each one.

"Animal patterns in a circus setting; insects in a garden; pearls in powder puff colors in among a feminine fluff of puffs and makeup containers."

The trailblazing display and marketing techniques for which her company is acclaimed shape how Carolee designs are sold today throughout the United States.

"I saw it all in my imagination first."

Imagination is a positive business force. Without imagination Peter and Kathie Davis never would have created IDEA.

"Peter and I came up with this idea in the middle of the night. At the time I was an aerobics instructor and he was a tennis coach at the University of California in San Diego. We had both graduated with degrees in physical education and business respectively and were newly married, wanting to work together. Friends of ours were making a living sending a newsletter to racket [tennis] stringers. Their newsletter inspired us to create our own for the exercise industry. Our newsletter included do's and don'ts, nutrition, anatomy, and choreography tips. Our original purpose was to help serve and educate aerobic instructors around the country."

They stayed up half the night talking about their idea, even imagining conventions stemming from this original concept. The very next day Peter quit his job at the University of California.

"I remember that our family and friends thought we were off our rockers. They called us a couple of daydreamers."

Imagination is not daydreaming. It is not fantasy. It is a tangible, useable force; a creative element in the advancement of individuals, families, and companies. Peter and Kathie Davis started selling subscriptions to their modest newsletter filled with information for aerobic instructors. Within five years they had developed standards for their industry and given birth to the finest aerobic certification program available today.

The newsletter was so well received that its subscribers wanted to hear and see more of the same. Peter and Kathie began planning their first convention for seven hundred people. Now, over ten years later, as many as ten thousand industry professionals attend IDEA's conventions and workshops throughout the year.

People who say they cannot get started until they have a decent brochure haven't talked to Peter and Kathie or Jim Rhode. Rhode started SmartPractice with no product and a lot of imagination.

"I listened to what dentists told me and let my imagination take it from there. For example, we are a major provider of stickers. Stickers that say, 'I flossed,' or 'I brushed today.' Then I got this idea that dentists should have a sticker club. The dentist would give each child three stickers. One for the child and two to trade. The idea came to me one day when I was sitting around a dentist's office."

Lane Nemeth gets ideas driving in her car.

"I saw this vision written on my car windshield. It said, 'We are a child development company. We are here to help parents raise their kids with self-esteem.' "

Nemeth said she realized that the toy, like the running shoe for Angel Martinez, was just the external symbol of something that went a lot deeper. She was frustrated, however, because at the time she did not feel Discovery Toys was doing enough to accomplish its true mission.

So she listed all the truths of self-esteem. Then she asked herself what products she could produce that would aid in teaching those truths to help change the planet.

"The first thing we did was create a parenting series of video, audio, and magazines to help parents develop self-esteem in their children. People are very busy today and don't have time to attend parenting seminars. So we bring this form of education to their doors."

I use the Problem-Cause-Effect-Cure Formula for channeling the output of my imagination into a workable structure.

Let's use Lane Nemeth's self-esteem example to show how we can use our imaginations to problem solve.

Problem: We are not being perceived as more than a toy company.

Cause: Not enough corporate or field effort to communicate Discovery Toys' true mission—to enhance children's self-esteem.

Effect: Image reflected is as a toy company rather than as child development experts.

Cure: List all the truths of self-esteem. Create, with the help of focus groups, a series of video, audio, and printed materials to help parents foster self-esteem in their children.

SLAYING DRAGONS

"I wonder what these people are *really* like. I can't relate to their perfect little lives." There is nothing worse than reading a book about so-called experts who do everything right. We want to get the message across in this book that each of us is capable of falling from grace.

I have made considerable progress north at those times when I have heard stories about how someone I truly admire failed. Others' efforts and perseverance in the face of failure and rejection have given me hope and motivated me to get off my duff and to quit feeling sorry for myself, and begin, again, to carry on.

When most of us fail, we feel extremely isolated. We cannot fathom, at least for a moment, that others could possibly fail to the degree we have failed. Hearing how people rebound from failure is energizing.

Lou Holtz says, "You find out what someone is really made of only after adversity has tested them."

John Crean says he hit bottom before he realized that staying debt-free was the only way to travel to the big time.

"In 1954 I was all but bankrupt—creditors chasing me down, the whole works. It came from too much success really quick. Spending money, running sportcars. I noticed something about myself and others who succeed. When success hits, that's the time we start screwing up. I was at the point of throwing in the towel; ready to go back to work for a trailer manufacturer.

"Then I started thinking, What did I do wrong? What happened here?"

He retraced his steps and realized he was doing things completely differently from how he did them at the beginning of his career.

"I used to buy and sell for cash because I had no credit. Now that I was a big shot and could borrow at any bank, I was getting deeper and deeper in debt.

"I also realized I was coasting. My product wasn't that good anymore and we couldn't demand cash payment. I began to reevaluate the whole operation. I slimmed down my staff, redesigned the product, and went back to a flat policy of never borrowing money."

Lane Nemeth recalls what her venture capitalist told her at the end of 1982, after she reached $10 million: "Now is the time all entrepreneurs fail. Historically it happens right around that 10 million mark. They cannot grow with the business. They need a CEO. The founder needs to stick with what he or she knows by staying out in the field and motivating the troops."

Nemeth said she did exactly what she was told to do: hired a CEO, got rid of her original management team (who she was told she had outgrown), and went out into the field to motivate.

"We grew from $10 to $25 million and lost $800,000."

Her bank pulled out and told her to go get more venture capital. She responded, "Over my dead body." Nemeth felt as if she had been hit by a car.

"I was in total shock. I remember staying up all night. I felt like giving up. But then I thought of the five thousand women that had stuck with me for years and my promise, if we all worked together, of success. I couldn't tell them I was quitting. I had to keep going for them as well as for myself."

Lane's original reason for creating Discovery Toys was connected closely with her desire to provide suitable toys for her infant daughter Tara. As a teacher she saw a great need for toys that were not only fun to play with, but safe and educational. Oddly enough, when the crisis hit Lane had a vision.

"I've always had two children—Tara and Discovery Toys. So I had this vision of Tara being in intensive care and my thinking, Well do I want to sell her or just let her die? At that moment I got up and realized that the answer was really very clear. Without question, I would sit in bed with Tara, hold on to her IV tubes, and influence her to stay alive in any way I could."

Lane was fired up again. She got herself out of bed, donned a business suit, went to the office, and fired her CEO.

"Everything was a nightmare that year. It was November and our computers broke down, so we didn't deliver December's orders. I got my staff together and told them we had no bank supporting us and we might not make it. Then we started cutting expenses, and I went out and found a temporary CEO who promised he would stay and help us out for two weeks. Then he stayed another two weeks, and that two weeks turned into a year. He eventually got us a bank loan and reinstalled our software.

"Bottom line is I am very optimistic. I just said to myself back then, 'It's got to get better. It can't get much worse.' Plus I am very creative and can always come up with a new way of looking at what others might consider a bleak situation."

In the mid-eighties, as Reebok's profits began doubling and tripling, Angel Martinez found himself exiled from the main office and on his way to California.

"I thought I was history. All my contributions at Reebok were being seriously questioned. Reebok was coming on strong in the marketplace, and so-called experts were being brought in to analyze and reassess."

Like Discovery Toys, Reebok was learning that nothing could kill success like success.

"It was a very difficult time for me. I questioned my self-worth when I should have been celebrating my accomplishments. But it was only after that burnout stage, when I was working for Reebok in California, that I experienced another renaissance in my work. It took concentration and awareness on my part, but I analyzed where I had been, and where, given my unique talents, I was capable of going."

After four years of building and maintaining a superb sales record, working eighteen-hour days, and beginning to feel the effects of burnout, Jim McMahon—the legendary Texas loan consultant who closes $50 to $60 million of loans each year, told me that he faced his own brand of reckoning:

"I went through a burnout time. It was not a slowdown in

production, but I was falling apart. My income was very good, and I would do whatever it took to keep the machine running.

"But none of us are bulletproof, and eventually we all have to realize that we are human. I knew I had better put my faith in a higher power and make sure my values were in place if I wanted to go long-term in my field."

Jim was working in his office on some nights until four o'clock in the morning. He was an athlete in college, but after four years selling loans, he found himself badly out of shape.

"That's when I sat back and realized there was nothing wrong with spreading my work to other people and focusing my day on what I was best at—delivering presentations and teaching people information."

When he began to delegate tasks, his volume doubled. He had more time at home and was able to get past the burnout hump.

By the late seventies Judi Missett was teaching twenty to twenty-five classes a week. She had an excellent reputation within a small niche in southern California, but she hadn't penetrated the larger market, nor did she feel she was headed in that direction.

"I was exhausted. I had nodes on my vocal cords and was losing my voice, and my body was drained by Friday of every week. It took me all weekend to bring my body and voice back so I could start teaching again on Monday."

Judi says, "I believe that messages and cues come to us, and if we listen we will know what the next step is that we must take. This breakdown of my body and spirit became an important message to me: You must do something different."

She decided she needed some help. She could have eliminated ten classes, but by letting go and delegating she broadened her market.

"I didn't know it then, but by letting go of my old ways I was allowing Jazzercise a chance to get into the big time."

I have had my share of personal and professional setbacks on the way to the promised land too. I know now I would not have changed a single experience which has created a deeper meaning in my life. I married when I was nineteen and had five children by the time I was twenty-seven.

Circumstances forced me to get a job when I was six months pregnant with my fifth child. The decision to enter the sales field was a smart one, but it was hard work and offered no shortcuts along the way. Though the career and the children weathered the struggles, my first marriage did not survive.

In the midst of becoming a single parent, more traumatic events occurred in my life: My sixty-two-year-old father died suddenly; three weeks later my grandfather died; six months later my thirty-six-year-old best friend died a shocking death.

When I first came up for air, I was numb, mostly bitter, and going through the robotic motions of a mother and sales-woman. I was a good actress and had the ability to hide my deep anger. I channeled all my energies into my children's activities and my career, showing the world I could make it on my own.

During an especially low period, I got a call from a prospective client to come over to her house and make a sales presentation. Her husband was a successful doctor in the community, and she had dedicated her adult life to him and the rearing of their four children. I can remember pulling into their driveway thinking how lucky they were to be part of such a perfect union. Little did I know I would soon hear a different story.

"My husband has just informed me he wants a divorce," she said with much bitterness in her voice. "I guess he's bored. Our children are all grown. I have no job skills. I have never balanced a checkbook in my life. And now I have to sell my beautiful home so I can go live in a condominium."

I was a different person when I walked out of her house. Her story was my personal wakeup call. This woman's bitterness oozed out of her, and I took it personally; I was afraid I was looking at my own unforgiving reflection.

I went home that night and looked around at my children,

feeling grateful once again. Not only could I balance my own checkbook, but I was a very good saleswoman who had the ability to hire or fire myself every single day of my life. Besides, I had the big family I'd always dreamt I'd have.

I thought about my other children, who were always planning new places we could travel as a family. For the first time in a long time I knew I was part of a real family, in spite of being a single parent. A "real" family has only one criterion — love.

All of that death and resurrection happened in my life well over fifteen years ago. I remarried in 1980, to a great man and single father of two children. Five years later we had a child together, Kathleen, a blessing in every way. Today we are business partners and the parents of eight wonderful children.

The burnout in my life was the death of an old self. I am no longer afraid to face the little deaths and resurrections of the self as I travel north. I am not afraid to face my own beastliness.

We all are part beauty and part beast. We, the teachers in this book, do not deny the presence of any part of ourselves. We are willing to slay the dragons. We have passion, are driven with our own unique energy, and continue to head due north.

Chapter One Review

- Energy is what turns a nobody into a somebody.
- Be more interested in building a business than making one sale.
- Set your mental compass to north each morning, and stay on your path.
- Ask yourself each day, How did my passion translate into dollars today?
- Do not sleep too much.

- Do not confuse motion with progress.
- Never say die.
- Out of necessity comes invention.
- Forget about the outcome.
- Learn to live with uncertainty.
- Stress is created in your mind by your thoughts.
- Live in the present moment. It is the only moment you have.
- Wake up with certainty about your work every day.
- Learn to fly blind.
- Sell to serve others.
- Become aware, willing, and detached.
- You are only a slave to what you are unaware of.
- Be willing instead of defiant.
- Stay as debt free as possible.
- Do not acquire more debt in an effort to motivate yourself.
- You are a good work in progress—every job prepares you for the next stage of your career.
- Your life is a huge training ground.
- Become comfortable with fear.
- Fearful people are usually obsessed with outcomes.
- Learn from your last failing experience.
- It is the death of the entrepreneur to make a decision based on fear.
- Do not associate with negative people. They are frightened.
- People who are optimistic get to where they want to go.
- Optimistic people are easier to train.
- Talent without guts is a waste.
- Realize all you have is time.
- Time is the great equalizer.

- You find out what you are made of only when adversity tests you.
- Delegate.
- No one is bulletproof.

THE AUTHENTIC IMAGE

" 'Real isn't how you are made,' said the Skin Horse. 'It's a thing that happens to you.' "

—e.e. cummings, THE VELVETEEN RABBIT

CREDIBILITY IS the bedrock of image. It cannot be bought at a public relations firm or from an image consultant. Because credibility is born of virtue, I went searching for stories about decent people doing the right thing.

When John Crean was a young venetian blind salesman, he had a competitor who was reputed to be hardworking for landing one of the toughest accounts in the business. Crean later found out that his competitor was paying off the company president to get orders.

"I refused to buy my way into that company. Eventually my competitor was found out, bankrupted his own company, and landed in jail. But for a period of time, other people's perception of what he stood for—hardworking and aggressive—was a more impressive image than mine."

VIRTUES AND VALUES

It was John Crean's values that caused him to stop making sales calls to a company where payoffs were expected. His integrity was reflected in his conduct. Good conduct stems from virtue. Virtue may seem old-fashioned and outdated, but it's virtue that creates an everlasting image.

In an advertising campaign, Oregon-based Columbia Sportswear portrayed owner Gert Boyle as the "scowling Mother Gert." Gert's son Tim, president of Columbia, along with almost everyone who knows her, will tell you that Gert Boyle is certainly a mother and a grandmother, but far from cantankerous. Some say she could be one of the softest touches in the Pacific Northwest.

Mother Gert may be different in life than her image projects, but both her image and her real self have one thing in common: shared values. The campaign gimmick had Ms. Boyle's blessing because it communicated a strong message: the customer deserves and receives the best at Columbia Sportswear.

Dynacom's Allan Gibby values the virtue of sincerity, an integral part of his image.

"Phoniness is one of the easiest things to see in a person, but for some reason many salespeople think the customer is very stupid. Salespeople think so-called image builders can make up for a lack of sincerity. No sales tool, car, or suit can take the place of honesty."

I met dozens of honest people when I spoke at the United Consumers Club (UCC) convention. It's a "members only" buying club that eliminates the middle man and allows the customer to buy directly from the manufacturer. I interviewed sales manager Rod Troutman, who passed on a story about UCC's founder, Jim Gagan. Gagan is a super salesman and a fanatic about honesty. He has built a company image around his favorite virtue—honesty—by recruiting franchise owners of high moral character. Troutman faxed me an interview with Gagan which explained why UCC's founder was so adamant about the truth.

"I learned an important lesson about honesty fast and early. When I was seventeen years old, I was hired as a messenger in

Chicago at a design firm named after Raymond Lowey, the designer of the Studebaker car. This was the first new car design from Detroit since World War II had ended.

"Mr. Lowey owned two new Studebakers which were parked in the garage of the Drake Hotel across the street from our building. I used one of them for running errands and delivering packages. This was the time when the entire world was insane for cars, and all of a sudden, I found myself driving this unbelievable car.

"Every time I stopped, people would gather around the car and ask questions about it. I was already known at the Drake Hotel, and all I needed to say to the attendant was 'I'll take one of the Raymond Lowey cars,' and it was mine. I took great pride in this privilege.

"On one occasion I didn't bring the car back until early the following morning. Nobody said a word. The next week, I had the car for two evenings in a row, and by the end of the month, it had become routine.

"I would cruise my neighborhood with the car and have a lot of fun. One evening while I was out cruising, Raymond Lowey, the car's owner, came into town. Mr. Lowey headed to the garage of the Drake for one of his cars. However, the office manager had taken out the other car, and the garage was empty of Studebakers. It soon came out that I had taken the car and had been using it every night. I lost my job, but was taught the virtue of honesty early in life."

Lane Nemeth has been criticized for her insistence on making toys that last. Longevity in the toy industry? Many manufacturers count on their toys falling apart in order to sell more.

"Our goal is to provide parents with toys that last for years. Based on what parents report to the company sales force, a toy from Discovery Toys is frequently handed down from child to child."

Probably no other product in America is older than Tootsie Roll. Usually when a product reaches an age advanced enough to be known as a "national institution," it bears little resemblance to its original form. When Leo Hirschfield hand-rolled the first Tootsie Roll in 1896, he insisted on wrapping it in a clean and sanitary paper. He named the candy after his little daughter Tootsie because his thoughts wandered to her as he rolled the candy.

In spite of a depression the company grew. During World War II, Tootsie Rolls were one of the few candies that remained in production because of their "keeping" or long-lasting qualities.

Tootsie Roll, Inc., President Ellen Gordon told me, "Products have been added to the new line and new markets entered, but Tootsie Rolls' first consideration has always been the maintenance of quality and value. This high standard has made Tootsie Roll a favorite wherever it has been sold in its long and successful history. Our image is who we are."

At Danielle Kennedy Productions we only create image-building brochures and press materials based on my experience and track record. My experience proves I know what I am talking about when it comes to sales and motivation. We make truthful statements:

"I [Danielle Kennedy] sold more in ten years than most salespeople sell in a lifetime. I want to share that experience and prevent your team from making unnecessary mistakes."

My most important strengths come from within myself. When I build my external image on those strengths, my public relations efforts are successful. My company distributes image-building materials all over the world. I test this literature by going inward and asking myself the following questions:

How congruent is this product with my basic values?

For example, I am currently writing a book on juggling family and career. Because I have proven that a woman can successfully manage a career and family, I feel confident writing such a book and introducing it to the working parent's marketplace.

FIND YOUR PASSION AND BUILD YOUR IMAGE AROUND IT

Passion is the trademark of high-level performers. Passion converts more prospects, faster. Either our passion is present inside us, we go find it, or it finds us. Once it's discovered, it's easy to build our exterior image around it.

Younger adults always ask me about discovering their passion. If the prerequisite for great selling is knowing one's passion, what happens when we are not sure what our passion is? The question of finding one's passion comes up frequently in conversations with my own adult children, younger friends, and the people in my audiences. I was thrilled when some light was finally shed on the subject. Recently, on my way to the Grand Rapids airport, I stumbled on a perfect contributor to this book, a man who seemed to appear out of nowhere.

I was riding in the front seat of a shuttle with a twenty-three-year-old driver named John, a business student in a local college. Sitting in the backseat was another passenger by the name of John—John Barker, Jr., a thirty-year-old Indianapolis attorney who teaches lawyers how to use computers for legal research. We struck up a conversation and young John, the shuttle driver, listened intently as we discussed selling and the importance of passion in the sales process.

"How do you find your passion? I get worried I may never know what mine really is, or I may never get to do the thing I am passionate about doing," John the driver asked.

John Barker gave him a brilliant answer.

"Finding your passion is a convergence of circumstances. You have an interest in something, and then you go explore it. Unconsciously you begin to program yourself to perceive the ideas, words, music, or books that support your interest.

"When you make a choice to pursue an interest, it is almost as if the brain says to itself, Notice everything that supports this interest, and overlook everything that doesn't align with the idea.

"For example, if you have an interest in international trading, but know nothing about it, don't allow your lack of knowledge to thwart your pursuit of that interest. Instead dive in and learn. Soon you will notice a billboard with a toll free number informing you of a place to call to gain international trading information. Ideas start to follow. Opportunities present themselves. There is some kind of metaphysical rhythm in the universe that promotes your interest.

"The mind alters the environment, and the environment then alters us. We get input from everywhere. Suddenly we evolve into something new because we let one idea, one interest flow. This is how passion is created and it can happen anytime in life."

Egads! I could relate to everything he said. I thought about the idea for this book being built around unconventional sales types. Once my brain got tuned in, everywhere I went I met untypical salespeople. Passion was also a key philosophy I wanted to focus on in this book. When I input the word "passion" into my brain, passionate people and stories began falling at my feet. When I began dreaming of building a log cabin in Idaho, everywhere I traveled I saw log cabins. Every magazine on the newsstand had pictures of log cabins. Everybody I talked to loved log cabins.

I am thankful to John Barker, Jr., for his thoughts and insights on the discovery of passion. Passion, so often mistaken as a genetic bit of luck granted to the chosen few, now seems a more tangible and viable state to pursue.

Judi Missett found her passion when she was two years old. Her mother enrolled her in a dance class on the recommendation of a doctor. Judi was pigeon-toed, and the doctor felt that ballet lessons would aid in turning out her feet. The first time Judi went to class, something clicked:

"It had such an impact on me; I can still clearly remember the moment of pure bliss."

ed in Council Bluffs, Iowa. Her mother would drive
maha, Nebraska, to find teachers that could keep up
with Judi's rapid progression. By the time Judi was eleven, she
was teaching her own dance classes and organizing dance
recitals.

At fourteen Judi was dancing professionally, and at eighteen
she was accepted into the dance program at Northwestern
University in Chicago, where she would study under the jazz
master Gus Giordano. This then led her to New York and all
over the world in various touring companies.

"I loved the thrill of pleasing audiences, but what I really enjoyed was watching other people vicariously enjoy the kind of
moves I performed as a dancer. I imagined what it would be
like if the whole audience was dancing on stage with me.

"There is such a communication with movement, such a
joy. I wanted to recreate that with my students. I felt that this
was my mission in life. So I started teaching classes at Gus's
studio—Jazz Dance Chicago."

Angel Martinez was a cross-country runner in high school
and college. He had a goal when he graduated from college.

"I knew that success would only come for me if I was able
to translate my passion for running into a concrete way of making a living."

Fortunately, he possessed hard-earned sales skills.

"All through school I won bikes and trips for selling. I knew
that I could use my sales ability to communicate my love for
fitness. I never thought to myself, I am selling this guy
footwear so I can make a buck.

"I call that topical or surface-level selling. It's a very phony,
selfish way to go, and the customer can see through this brand
of selling a mile away.

"On the other hand, I was coming from a deep place within
myself. Running taught me how to cope with my life. I am forever indebted to running for the lessons it taught me. Therefore, I was living proof that the best investment a person could
make to change their life was to buy a pair of athletic shoes."

Martinez believes that he was selling part of himself.

"I walked in completely convinced that they must have what I could provide. This confidence and conviction comes from my passion."

Missett and Martinez wrapped their lives around what they were selling. None of us can be certain of the stage in our life when our passion will become clear.

When seven figure loan salesman Jim McMahon was ten years old, he won three bikes selling newspaper subscriptions. He continued to sell throughout his teens, and when he graduated from college he was ready for a sky's-the-limit opportunity to sell.

"I made a list of everything I wanted to do, and mortgage lending was not on it. Then a friend of mine told me about an opportunity to interview with a large mortgage company. It sounded very exciting, but I remember my wife wanting to kill me after learning it was a 100 percent commission job."

He had just found out she was going to have a baby.

"She told me I had ninety days to make a living as a loan officer, and if it didn't happen I'd better find another job. The pressure was on, but in the midst of that pressure I discovered my love and passion for selling loans."

By the time Jim was in the loan business for ninety days, he had closed over a million dollars' worth of loans, and received a paycheck that amounted to more money than he and his wife had seen in almost a year's worth of salaried work.

In Jim's case, his passion found him.

When she graduated from high school, Evelyn Echols never dreamed she'd be selling Al Steele and Joan Crawford a trip on a cruise line for their honeymoon. At graduation she took a trip to New York. She liked it so much she decided to stay and enroll in nursing school, a profession she had always intended to pursue.

"I soon decided that being a nurse was not for me. At first it was hard for me to face the fact I was not cut out to be one. I had planned on becoming a nurse for most of my young life.

Eventually, I had to admit to myself and to a lot of other people that I was mistaken.

"So I applied for a job at a worldwide advertising agency headquartered in New York. I got the job and was assigned to the travel division. This job put me in contact with the travel business and ultimately in touch with my passion. I eventually went to work for a travel agent and worked on straight commission. Once my clientele grew, I decided to open up my own travel agency."

Sometimes a passion appears in the form of a hobby or an extracurricular activity. Hollywood's former superagent Michael Ovitz graduated from UCLA with a degree in premed, hoping to please his father by becoming a doctor. But Ovitz picked up a passion for the entertainment industry working as a tour guide at Universal Studios and Twentieth Century Fox.

Allan Gibby held a video camera in the fifth grade when he was selected to videotape an assembly.

"I loved it, but by junior high school I had been steered away from it by peer pressure. It just wasn't cool to be a video monitor."

By the time he was twenty-one, the camera had found its way back into Gibby's hand.

Although I thrived in the sales industry, my real passion was performance. I chose a career in sales because of its performance quality. When I first entered the work force, I was in a financial crisis; I wanted to work independently and structure a schedule around my five children. Sales gave me that opportunity.

Once I passed through financial crisis and my track record in sales was well established, I was literally drafted into the speaking profession by my industry. Speaking for me was a pleasure and a passion I allowed myself in between sales. For many years I spoke for no fee, sharing all I learned from my own experiences in selling.

Sometimes we do not have the luxury of working with our passion because of financial reasons. John Crean started selling window blinds instead of recreational vehicles, which was his real love, because he did not have the capital to start on such a big scale.

"But I always knew what I was shooting for," says Crean.

Barry Kaye has probably sold more life insurance in the last thirty years than anyone else on this planet. If not the most, then awfully close. Author Bob Shook gave me his phone number for an interview.

"Don't pass this man up. Talk about fire in the belly, he's got it!"

Shook was right. Five seconds into the conversation I felt guilt-ridden because I didn't own enough life insurance. I asked him how he was able to earn millions of dollars in income each year for over thirty years in the life insurance business.

"Because I sell the most incredible product in the world—insurance. Look at it as a pure investment with a minimal amount of money. Whether you drop dead now or fifty years from now, you get paid big time. I work with wealthy people. They have junk money—money they don't need. Uncle Sam is going to take 55 cents of every dollar they have, and their kids are going to take 45 cents. Their income is in excess of what their lifestyle requires. These are the people that need to put their money into life insurance; otherwise the government is going to get it when they die."

There's no arguing with Barry, because he's deeply knowledgeable and fueled with a fire of passion. I asked him if he was born with a policy in his hand.

"Are you kidding? I started in radio and television in the late forties. I was in show business until 1960. Even worked for NBC. I was up for the Jack Paar show. It was between me and Johnny Carson. Prior to that audition I was one of the top ten disc jockeys in America. I came to California to do 'The Tonight Show,' but Carson got it and my career was over.

"I went into finance after that because I played the stock market and was pretty good at it. I got interested in insurance, not just any insurance, but insurance for affluent people. I started studying up on it, and it made so much sense. Why should these people die and give all their money to the government? Their kids should get it. It's such a waste to see all this discretionary money sit there and get taxed. Why don't people see this?

"This bothered me so bad that in 1962 I joined New England Life, and in my first year I practically broke all records in the history of the business. By 1965 I had my own insurance company."

There's no telling how anyone may end up finding his or her passion. Most people would have stayed home and cried in their beer if they lost out on "The Tonight Show." Barry Kaye was already proving John Barker's passion theory right. Barry turned a new interest into a passion. Today he owns $23 million worth of insurance.

Once our passion is found, the next challenge lies in creating ways to shamelessly tell the world why our product or service is a necessity. We communicate that message through virtuous acts. Seven figure folk consider such acts part of authentic image building.

KEEPING PROMISES CREATED THE NUSKIN GENERATION

I flew to Provo, Utah, to meet the owners of NuSkin. They have in excess of 300,000 distributors, a distribution center that is the size of five football fields, and the owners are barely forty years old, running a debt-free company. I couldn't wait to lay my eyes on these miracle workers.

Blake Roney, Sandie Tillotson, Steven Lund and other shareholders keep their promises. They promised one another always to put their distributors first. Sandie had lost precious time and money in her former life at a multilevel marketing company that filed bankruptcy. In the early years at NuSkin, she and the other owners refused to pay themselves a salary.

Their willingness to pay their distributors on time, and to create "all of the good, none of the bad" in over one hundred personal care products has paid off big time. NuSkin is one of the largest contributors to the Utah economy, and NuSkin's superior image is reflected in the class of people they recruit into their organization.

Prominent NuSkin distributor Mary Averill, a Harvard MBA, was formerly a vice president of a bank. Her husband, Bud Corkin, is a lawyer and a former assistant attorney general for the state of Massachusetts.

Hung-Tai Wang was a research chemist for the U.S. Department of Defense who became a distributor in 1988. In the beginning he wrestled with his career change. He was fearful that his devotion to science and his scientific way of thought would conflict with the profit-making personality stereotypes that supposedly lurked in the multilevel marketing arena. Instead the positive nature of the NuSkin people began to attract him. In 1990 he resigned from the U.S. government and became a full-time distributor. Today he ranks among the peak performers at NuSkin.

Dr. Wang says, "If there is a lesson to be learned from my achievements, it is the importance of leadership. Network marketing is driven by leaders."

Other top distributors include Kathy and Craig Bryson, the parents of eleven children, who had enough faith in themselves and NuSkin to leave salaried jobs.

David Clifton left the Houston police force after thirteen years.

Martha Lowrey was a cleaning lady, and her husband was a trim carpenter when they joined the company.

The Blue Diamonds are an important part of the NuSkin image. These salespeople are NuSkin's six and seven figure giants, photographed for major corporate advertising and promotional efforts. They get all the glory, and that is exactly how President Blake Roney wants it.

"Myself and other members of Corporate are merely the janitors. We built our company around the needs of the people we serve—our distributors in the field."

STREET SMART IMAGE BUILDING

Shirley Pepys and I met thirty years ago when we were both young mothers trying to make a living selling out of our homes. Shirley proved that mothers know how to sell. She sold infant seat covers out of her garage. Today her $30 million company, NoJo, Inc., is one of the most successful manufacturers of juvenile products in the world.

"We've always gone out into the street and asked our customers what they wanted from us next. Even our image is based on what they ask for. My oldest daughter, Renee, is my vice president of sales and marketing. She formed an Executive Sales Rep Council consisting of five NoJo sales representatives. Through our executive council's annual meetings, the company learns more about what our customers need."

RELIABILITY HAS EVERLASTING INFLUENCE

Publicist Linda Fields put me in touch with Dr. Sharon D'Orsie, scientist turned saleswoman and president of Eagle Environmental Health. Dr. D'Orsie is an extraordinary combination of super saleswoman and scientist.

Sharon recalls having a prospect—a chemical company—that needed technical assistance as well as help getting a program organized. Sharon spent an inordinate amount of time with the chemical company's safety man, helping him figure out a way to approach the problem.

"I wrote this up in a very detailed proposal that really gave him the benefit of the years of my experience. When it came time to do the work, he gave the job to someone who bid a lower price. I was disappointed, but I kept in contact.

"Later on I found out he had a heart attack, and I made a point of sending him some funny cards. About a year after our first encounter, he called me up and said, 'We made a terrible mistake when we selected that other firm to do the work, and now we want to ask you to work with us.' Who knew the earlier disappointing experience would contribute to my credibility?"

Publicist Linda Fields insisted I meet another of her clients: David Steitz, the CEO of Characters, Inc., Houston's largest full-service supplier of prepress, prepublishing, and presentation graphics. He gave me some sound image-building advice too:

"Our image equals going the extra mile."

Steitz built his image by reinforcing the idea in the marketplace that his company was the place to go when no one else knew how to do the job.

"We were finishing up a financial report one time and it was due to be delivered on Sunday morning. We knew that we were delivering copies to the CEO and the CFO. We could have easily used a driver or a delivery service.

"I chose to deliver the package myself. That sent a message to the customer that their project was a priority and was in responsible hands. Small gestures of reliability created our image."

COSTUMING YOUR IMAGE

I wanted to get my seven figure friends' opinion on dressing for success. It has always been a touchy subject for me. When I was breaking sales records in the seventies, my sales manager called me into his office to give me some image advice.

At the time I drove a station wagon and considered myself well groomed. However, in spite of my six figure salary, I had five mouths to feed, and a potpourri of music, dance, and art lessons to finance. The money went fast, but to an excellent cause.

I never thought twice about driving vice presidents or sheiks around in my conservative car. My customers were happy, and I had referrals coming out of my ears. None of my customers ever told me to go home and change my clothes because I wasn't wearing a certain label. So it really hurt when my manager said,

"You really should be wearing more expensive clothes. And that car! Why don't you buy a luxury car? After all, you are the top producer in this office and you have an example to set."

He never praised me for taking new salespeople out on sales calls. Nor did he notice all the testimonial letters I received from satisfied customers. Worse, he was a married man who was having affairs with several of the so-called smartly dressed saleswomen in our office, and our entire sales force knew it.

I wanted to ask him what kind of an example he thought he was setting, but I bit my tongue. If I had asked him, I'm sure he would have said, "A good one." After all, he was wearing an Armani suit.

"I think of dressing for success as costuming," says David Steitz.

"Wouldn't it be nice if you could walk into a sales presentation in shorts and a T-shirt and everybody in the room who was wearing pin-striped suits couldn't care less about what you were wearing? They would immediately take you for who you really are—an honest, forthright, dynamic salesman who delivers the goods, in spite of the fact that you look somewhat sloppy at the moment.

"The problem with not concerning yourself with the costuming of the event you are attending, in this case the sales presentation that may land you the million dollar account, is you immediately make it the concern of the prospects.

"Dress in a manner that makes the customer feel comfortable. If he is dressed to the nines and you look like you are about to go play golf, your choice of clothing has become an issue. And the point should be that you dress in order to make your clothes a nonissue," Steitz advises.

David will oftentimes wear an open shirt and a pair of khaki pants to work. On those occasions he may be meeting with some of the creative people from a company, and his choice of dress would be considered appropriate.

"Or maybe it is Friday and I am headed over to Compaq Computer, where it is their blue jeans day."

Shirley Pepys is a fanatic about proper costuming because details are very important in the building of the NoJo image.

"One small detail, like a sales rep wearing some goofy hat because they think it is cute and interesting, is totally inappropriate. It immediately takes the focus off of what is important."

She is a stickler for detail in her displays at toy shows and in the retail arena as well.

"This is what has set us apart. The way we display our products. We have learned a lot from Ralph Lauren and Liz Claiborne. Their presentations are breathtaking. We want our reps, our displays, and our entire package to present that same polished image."

John Marconi, president of Orange Coast Title Insurance Companies, believes simplicity is important in terms of costuming.

"I caution my people about the way they dress and what they drive. I have watched outstanding sales reps begin to make big money and start wearing the expensive watches and driving the fancy cars around the same customers who watched them come up from nothing.

"Then, to make matters worse, success seems to spoil them. They forget to deliver the service that made them successful.

And suddenly the customer says, 'Hey, this guy is making a fortune off my business.'

"The secret is not to outdistance the very customer base that you are counting on. You can be a leader of people, but not a king."

Carolee Friedlander says, "Your inner attitude is manifested outwardly by what you wear. Dress is important, but only from the standpoint that it's done in good taste to build on a respectful image.

"You won't see us wearing miniskirts, hiking boots, or piercing our belly buttons. The Carolee image is classic and authentic. Our people must go beyond just looking the part. They are the part."

Maryles Casto, owner of one of the most successful travel agencies in the world, Casto Travel, says,

"Image is *not* about clothes. My agents wear uniforms. I want them to be clean, tailored-looking, and professional. Our dress code accomplishes that goal. The uniform shows pride in who we are, and this pride is part of our image. My people are seen in airports wearing green uniforms and buttons that have our service credo written on it.

"Our message is that we take pride in our work. Plus the uniform solves other problems. Because their mind is not on how they look, my people can feel confident that they are presenting themselves in a good light and can concentrate on what the customer is thinking and feeling. When they wear a Casto Travel uniform, they draw people's attention to their behavior, placing a heavy responsibility on each of them."

She says the decision to wear a uniform, an expensive suit, a simple dress, or casual slacks and a shirt depends on two questions:

How comfortable are you wearing certain clothing in the presence of the customer?

What is the unspoken dress code of your industry?

I can recall misjudging one of my lecture audiences and selecting a completely inappropriate outfit. I was the opening keynote speaker for a group of two thousand bankers and their spouses. I chose a black evening suit which was slightly off the shoulders. As soon as I walked into the crowd I felt the stares. I knew it was too sexy, and not businesslike enough for that crowd. Also, I had very long, bushy hair. My hair in combination with my suit distracted the group, making my warm-up session with that audience twice as long as it normally is when dress is not an issue.

In the entertainment world superagent Michael Ovitz schmoozes with Fortune 500 executives, Wall Street financiers, and studio heads in suits that one advertising executive says "probably cost more than my Buick."

Knowing our territory is the best solution to our image-building decisions.

Allan Gibby admits he hates wearing a suit.

"I am a very casual dresser, and luckily I work in sports production, where everyone else is casual too. When I first started Dynacom, I read all the books about dressing for success. On my first presentation I decided to wear a suit. I felt so uncomfortable that I haven't worn one since.

"I hope someday business will judge people more on who they are than what they wear. I know too many people who have financed their way into debt because they thought they could wear an image."

Peter and Kathie Davis don't feel comfortable walking around "overdressed" at their fitness conventions because "All of the instructors are wearing their aerobic attire, and we have no desire to differentiate ourselves from them. We are there for our instructors and want all the participants to feel comfortable coming up to us and discussing their issues."

However, on normal business days at the office, Peter Davis says,

"Lately we specify only Fridays for casual dress. We used to let people dress casual every day, but Kathie and I began to notice the staff becoming a bit too casual about other aspects of their jobs. Plus many visitors, such as sponsors, come into our headquarters, and we didn't want to feel underdressed around them or make them feel overdressed. People have a tendency not to take you as seriously when your appearance is less than professional."

The Levi Company has done an excellent job of promoting "Dress Down Fridays," and many companies have given in to the pressure from employees to dress casually.

Jim Rhode worries that if this movement gets out of hand it could turn into another example of atrophy in the professional setting.

"Right or wrong we are judged by how we look. So at our company we are committed to looking very stylish and well dressed."

What is considered underdressing in one industry may be just fine in another.

Nowadays I always ask myself,

What can I wear that makes me feel confident? If I put something on that makes me feel uncomfortable or self-conscious, I block my energy and passion, which are the keys to a successful presentation.

GOOD MANNERS AND CREATIVE ENTERTAINING IDEAS

John Marconi believes good manners are as important to an image as proper dress. He remembers an incident that happened when he was a brand-new salesperson. His sales manager called him into his office for a little pep talk.

"He was sitting in his chair and I was sitting across from him. He had his feet up on the desk, and the only thing that he was letting me look at was the bottom of his shoes.

"This man was trying to sell me on the importance of hard work. The message he was sending me, however, was one of laziness. I seemed to mean nothing to him since the only thing he was letting me stare at was the bottom of his shoes. Over the last twenty-five years, I have never lost sight of that image."

Socializing with dentists contributes to the success of Jim and Naomi Rhode's business.

"There is a magic about being with people around food. We entertain at our home, and our dentist friends from all around the country come and have dinner with us. They talk about it for years. When we run into them years later, the thing they remember and bring up first is the fact that we entertained them at our home. They interpret this as a very caring gesture."

Rhode finds it easier to establish intimacy in his own home. He never forgets the clients and their homes that he has been entertained in, and feels this hospitality in his home leaves the clients with similar good feelings. Dentists are more at ease and open in his home. They are willing to answer questions, which seem to come up more naturally, such as, "What are you buying out of our catalog that you hope we never stop selling?"

Planning unique social events with big-time clients creates lasting memories. One organization I spoke for rented one of the most beautiful theaters in America for the evening to benefit its clients. An intimate candlelight dinner for under fifty people was served on the stage. The evening had a *Phantom of the Opera* theme. Everyone was given a mask and a collector's plate, and during dinner the guests were entertained by cast members from the *Phantom* road show. They sang favorite selections and enacted short scenes. At the end of the evening each couple had their picture taken with the Phantom. Evenings like that create everlasting positive images in a client's mind.

RESPECT CREATES THE MAGIC

Edie Fraser, President of Public Affairs Group, Inc., and a member of the Committee of 200, says when she first started her business, she thought image and self-promotion were the most important keys to her future success. Today, however, she believes the key factor in her success has been the permanent attainment of her customers' respect.

Helen Gurley Brown says making it to the big time occurs when "you gain the respect of the customer through little things like being punctual, quiet, persevering, and extremely knowledgeable about your customers' business needs. You cannot just go in and be friendly and count on your good looks and pretty clothes. Your product has to be presented as something that can enhance the life of your customer."

Helen believes follow-up with clients has had a lot to do with how much respect these clients have for you in the long term. Even when a prospect says, "We're not interested in your services right now," that prospect will respect you by answering, "I am going to call you in exactly two weeks or two months, just to make sure you haven't changed your mind."

Heida Thurlow claims her follow-up persistence was her special virtue in her early selling days.

"I would not take no for an answer. Prospects would give me a 100 percent unshakeable no. Then I would call on them again after a month, and without hesitation they were saying yes. I, like many other buyers, had been guilty of the same indecisiveness and fluctuation. In my own life I would oftentimes give people a quick no, and then after I had a little time to think about it, I would change my mind and decide to buy. If the salesperson doesn't go back, she never gives the customer a chance to change his or her mind."

Helen Gurley Brown says, "You must never lose your gumption, and when you don't, you gain the respect of those you serve. I am still making selling calls and "asking for the order." Recently I had lunch with the business editor of the *New York Times* to whom I pitched a story about *Cosmo* I thought she might consider running in the *Times*. She is a good person, and we had a terrific lunch, but she turned me down. Who knows? She may do the story later."

Carolee Friedlander remembers the early years with her vendors as being very tough.

"My company was just me in the beginning—me working out of my kitchen, then me working out of a little studio I built in my backyard. When I would go to Rhode Island, where all the buyers were, I was eventually given a chance at their business because they came to respect my seriousness and the quality of the work I was producing.

"I did not have a big fancy image to fall back on. My image was created by my seriousness to do good work. The decision makers picked up on that and gave me a chance in those very early days. Winning the respect of giants like Bloomingdale's—over fifteen years ago—has created longtime and very loyal relationships with their people and mine.

"You meet the same people going up the ladder as you do coming down. How you treat them, and the promises that you make and keep, are all factors that can make or break a respectful relationship. At Carolee we are proud to say that we have been doing business with the same vendors for the past fifteen years, which translates into a very credible image."

Carolee believes you build respect with the customer by communicating, in a highly self-confident manner.

"Self-confidence is not an arrogance, but a strength that comes from doing homework. We try to get that message across. Whenever I stray from that image, by hiring people who are different than we are, it never works out."

Josie Natori's biggest challenge when she began Natori Lingerie was transferring her reputable and respected image as a Wall Street stockbroker to one as a respected entrepreneur in the retail world.

"Respect is the result of passion. You cannot expect to get respectful reactions from people if what you are doing doesn't originate from deep within your soul.

"I am a natural saleswoman. I come from the Philippines, where being a woman entrepreneur is very commonplace.

Women are always selling something, from the time they are very young. It comes very natural to me.

"I began playing the piano at the age of four, and by the time I was nine years old, I was a concert pianist. A good pianist creates the music from the inside of her soul and then it comes out through the fingers. Selling is the same way. If you sell from deep within yourself, your image with the customer will also run deep."

Josie says when she left Wall Street she had accomplished everything she set out to do there, and there was no more energy coming out of her for that career. She wanted to get into the lingerie business, and she knew she would succeed because the desire came from deep within.

"I began building an image because I was on fire from within. I was doing what I wanted to do again. For many years I felt that way on Wall Street, but when the feelings were no longer there, I left. The reason many salespeople no longer get respect from their clients is that they no longer respect what they do or themselves for doing it. Always use your inner life as your guide to building a respectable image."

THE APPROACHABLE IMAGE

"Now that I am an entrepreneur, my clientele includes those who work for me. It is very important that I am accessible to all of my people," says Heida Thurlow.

"If a girl from the assembly line wants to come into my office and talk to me, she knows I will be there for her. When people think of Heida Thurlow, I want them to think of someone who is approachable and easy to talk to. I also feel being a mother has helped me become very nurturing. A nurturing, approachable image is one I have tried to foster from the beginning."

Recently Jim Rhode came into his office at 9:00 A.M. and never made it to his desk until 4:00 P.M. that same afternoon.

"Being accessible to my people is what keeps my pulse on the business. I know who my customers are—our end users, the health care professionals, and my staff. Paperwork takes a backseat to these people. My people tell me I have an uncanny ability to solve a problem, but I think I developed that attribute over time by making myself available to those I serve."

Carolee continues to visit stores and make personal appearances whenever her schedule permits.

"I never want to forget how I got to where I am. I know plenty of people who quit making personal appearances once they became extremely successful. I think that is a big mistake. I want my customers to be able to talk to me about anything for two reasons: It is part of the quality service our company offers, and it keeps me in touch with the marketplace.

"Whenever I go out to the stores, I ask myself, What are we doing better than our competition? and What is our competition doing better than us? The day our company stops asking these two questions is the day our company image will break down dramatically."

Approachable people usually have a reputation for being excellent listeners. The best thing a salesperson can do is to listen intently to the customer. A customer's deepest desire is to be heard. A customer who trusts that I am a good listener will spread good rumors to reinforce my positive image.

Being accessible put William Wrigley in the big time. He started out as a soap salesman, failing miserably because no one would buy his soap. As an incentive he decided to give a piece of spearmint gum away to any customer who would buy his soap. His customers told him to forget about the soap and start selling the gum. The rest is history.

A CARING IMAGE

Superagent Michael Ovitz mixes business with friendship and according to *Businessweek* "follows up with a list of 100 movers and shakers who he calls every couple of weeks whether or not he is doing business with them. When Wall Street financier Theodore J. Forstmann was in the hospital for an operation to fix a sinus blockage, Ovitz called him regularly and sent him videos to keep him entertained. The two have never done a deal, but both hold the door open to future ventures."

Helen Gurley Brown says there is something very charming about people who listen well, speak tactfully, and truly care about the customer.

"When you care about something or someone, you almost involuntarily start selling. That is why I think selling permeates our lives. Caring parents sell their kids on the benefits of being good students and responsible people. When a man or woman falls in love, they each try to sell themselves to the other person."

Judi Sheppard Missett feels it is our responsibility to care. Only those who care are hired at Jazzercise. That is the one personality trait they look for when interviewing instructors.

"It is not just about dance ability. It is about being caring and unintimidating. Too many times in this industry the instructor is very threatening—gorgeous body and a bit too self-confident.

"We can't forget that our customer may be a thirty-five-year-old housewife who has gained five additional pounds with each new baby. She doesn't need to spend her hour out of the house being intimidated by an instructor who looks down her nose at her."

Judi wants fitness to become as available to people as the McDonald's hamburger. In order to achieve that goal, the Jazzercise image must welcome people who normally would shy away from exercise.

"We train people to care. Little things such as birthday cards, notes praising progress, and special get-togethers have created a very caring atmosphere here. There is no room for instructors whose sole purpose is to show off their bodies."

People who care generate loyalty among their customers.

During the 1994 Los Angeles earthquakes, L.A. Cellular Phone Company donated over one thousand cellular phones to the rescue team. Disc jockey Rick Dees heard about it and said over the air, "I am not product loyal until I hear something like this."

Nobody cared more than Walt Disney. He was obsessed about making products the customers would buy.

Disney once said, "The inclination of my life has been to do things and make things which will give pleasure to people."

When a salesperson loves what he or she does, is good at doing it, and deeply cares in the process, it makes it very difficult for a competitor to win. Is there a better image than that to communicate to the public?

MEMORY ENHANCES IMAGE

Fifty years later Dale Carnegie's classic book *How to Win Friends and Influence People* still offers some of the best image-building advice on the market today: Use the power of our memory. How can we care if we don't remember a name, a face, or an experience? If we have a problem remembering, we should take a course to help ourselves overcome our handicap.

From an early age my late father taught me the importance of having a good memory.

"When you forget a name or any detail of a story that is important to someone you care about, you might as well slap that person in the face.

"On the other hand when you run into a client years later and can remember a name, specifics from a conversation, or details from a certain event, that customer feels valued."

He taught me to remind my customers just how good my memory is at every chance I get. It is not only flattering, but it shows I can be trusted to remember information, facts, and details. If that isn't image building, what is?

Chapter Two Review

- Credibility is the bedrock of image.
- Virtue creates an everlasting, positive image.
- Sincerity is an integral part of an authentic image.
- A fancy car or a designer suit cannot take the place of honesty.
- Your image is who you are.
- The maintenance of quality and value creates image.
- Your most important strengths come from within yourself.
- Product and service must be congruent with your basic values.
- Passion is the trademark of high-level performance.
- Build your image around your passion.
- Your image evolves from the pursuit of your passion.
- Translate your passion into a concrete way of making a living, and success will follow.
- A confident image comes from the presence of passion in the personality.
- You cannot be sure when your passion will appear. Be alert.
- Image involves creating ways to shamelessly tell the world why your product or service is a necessity.
- While formulating image, ask your customers what they want from you next.
- Reliability has an everlasting influence.
- Image means keeping in contact with the customer.
- Image means being known for going the extra mile.
- Small gestures of reliability create image.
- Dress in a manner that makes the customer feel comfortable.

- There is a difference between being interested in the customer and acting interesting in front of the customer.
- Never try to outdistance your customer materially.
- Dress simply and in good taste.
- Image is not about clothes.
- Know the unspoken dress code of your industry.
- You are not better than your customers.
- Your appearance must be professional.
- Good manners are important.
- Plan unique social gatherings.
- Respect creates the magic with customers.
- Be approachable.
- Care about those you serve.
- Remember.

THE SCIENCE OF SEVEN FIGURE RESULTS: SELLING MORE PROSPECTS; OPENING MORE NEW MARKETS

"The entire population is my market, until proven otherwise."
— LANE NEMETH, CEO, DISCOVERY TOYS

THE DIFFERENCE between earning five, six, or seven figure incomes in sales is the addition of more prospecting activity and the addition of previously untapped markets.

"The conventional salesperson doesn't prospect enough. It's the hours that count, and people don't put in the time. If I work nineteen hours and you work eight hours, I have twice the experience you do. I have only been selling insurance for thirty-six years, but I have a hundred years of experience," says Joe Gandolfo.

"Too many salespeople eliminate a possible market just because they presume prematurely. You don't know where you stand until you ask. The worst thing that can happen is some-body might say no," says Discovery Toy President Lane Nemeth.

Judi Sheppard Missett knows no boundaries either. She and her husband packed up and left Chicago in the early seventies and moved to California, the health mecca of the world, which promised to be ripe with prospective Jazzercisers.

Jenny Craig jumped on a plane back in 1982 and flew to Australia because she knew that her weight loss program would be unique in the Australian marketplace. Americans were already inundated with such programs, but Australia was just beginning to conduct nutrition symposiums and become more fitness conscious.

"We opened fifty locations in twelve months. That would have been unheard of in the United States," says Jenny Craig.

GLOBAL DOOR-KNOCKERS

Who would believe that Joe Gandolfo, Judi Sheppard Missett, Lane Nemeth, and Rich Luisi—the sales hall of famers—are just a few of our seven figure door knockers? Twenty-five years later the thought of getting hurt by people who made fun of my door-knocking efforts really galls me. Unknowingly, I was performing one of the most brilliant prospecting activities. Even today, sales gurus teach people that door knocking is a waste of time. May all those who listened to such nonsense, and missed out on a lucrative niche, forgive their ill-advisors.

"The first year my ratios were low," says Joe Gandolfo, who door-knocked young couples, athletes, and students on the Louisiana State University campus.

"I'd call on two hundred people and maybe get fifteen ap-pointments. Each succeeding year my ratios got better and bet-ter."

What about rejection?

"So what? I learned to handle rejection on an athletic field. It's part of the game, part of life. The sun rises in the east and sets in the west. I was basically spreading the word. Never even discussed insurance on the first go around. 'Hi, I'm Joe Gandolfo, and I just wanted to stop by to see if I could come by next week to discuss a super opportunity with you.'

"Then I would just leave the rest in God's hands."

Door knocking was my only option when I launched my sales career. I got plenty of flack from the naysayers—those salespeople in the office I used to call the quicksand crowd, who would moan because the coffee was cold or there wasn't any toner in the copy machine.

They'd whisper in my ear: "Stick around here. Eat a donut. The phones will be ringing off the hook real soon."

Many salespeople prejudge certain niches and unknowingly cut off opportunities to earn their way to a seven figure future.

I asked Rich Luisi, the legendary salesperson over at Electrolux, what he thinks about door knocking.

"Nothing takes the place of hands-on door knocking. People think it doesn't work anymore. That's fine with me because I have twenty-five hundred salespeople out doing the same thing I did for twenty-five years, and it's working for them as well as it did for me. I demonstrated over thirty thousand cleaning systems by simply knocking on doors. Phones and faxes are fine, but more than ever customers crave human contact."

Door knocking and cold calling weren't beneath insurance sales wiz Lin Lam either.

"I wrote over a million dollars' worth of policies the first year in the insurance business by door knocking businesses all day in Chinese neighborhoods. My first prospect, the owner of the Gaslight Motel in Buena Park, California, is still an excellent customer."

Lin says salespeople give rejection too much attention.

"You have to be courageous and bold. If someone said, 'Get

out,' or 'No, thanks,' I wanted to know why. I'd say to them, 'Do you have perfect insurance? You don't need anyone to examine your policy to make sure it is the best for you? Did you ever consider I can tell you some things you do not know?' "

Door knocking was as natural as dancing for Judi Missett too.

"I had my ten-year-old daughter, my nieces and nephews, and myself all door-knocking the neighborhood. We placed Jazzercise door hangers on people's front doors. Today we are an international company in over thirty-four countries, but door-knocking neighborhoods all over the world is one of the ways we have always found the right prospects."

While out door knocking Judi continued to find out things about her prospects and found out why some people she talked to were not good candidates for prospects. Child care was becoming a problem, so she began to offer it to her students, and this offering doubled her clientele.

"But if I hadn't been door knocking, I never would have found out what their objections were. Their objections allowed me to fill a need, and as a result I expanded my market."

MULTIPLE PERSONALITIES, MULTIPLE NICHES

We made it to seven figure status by broadening our base of prospecting and not succumbing to a single-niche marketing habit. Sure, it can be a temptation when a particular niche pulls some fast money, but it's also dangerous. We become attached to working just one niche and then we become a pest.

For me door knocking, cold calling, past customer calls, social-centers-of-influence contacts, and past life acquaintances (grade school, high school, etc.) were just a few of the niches I tapped regularly.

I am glad I never got stuck in one niche and neglected other prospecting avenues, or believed trainers who said certain forms of prospecting did not work. Those authorities never prospected the niche long enough to reap the rewards. Some niches have quicker payback times than other niches. The secret is to tap them all.

I found the quickest payback was the past customer niche. I could make five past customer calls and always count on at least one new name to come in during each prospecting session. If I was in a slump, I would always start with the past customer niche or the social centers of influence niche to get my business development activated again.

Judi Missett explored dozens of niches.

"I figured I needed to go to the places that people go— YWCAs, meeting halls, comunity centers, and recreation departments. I knew there I would be able to find the kind of person I wanted to market to."

She prospected newspapers and convinced them to do articles about her new, fun way of getting fit.

"I had good publicity pictures because I had been in the theatre, and I had an interesting story to tell. When I called on the newspaper people, I already had most of the story or press release written, as well as the professional photos. Reporters love it when you walk in prepared, because it makes their job so much easier."

The papers would run full-page stories about Judi and her new Jazzercise classes, and she started packing in the students.

Dr. Sharon D'Orsie found her niche at trade association meetings. She is active in the American Industrial Hygiene Association, the American Society of Safety Engineers, and the Air and Waste Management Association.

"I take positions, run for offices, write columns, chair events, do special projects, and really work hard for these groups. What happens when you do this is you become very well connected, and for me it has led to landing a lot of big accounts."

Sharon tells young salespeople:

"Get used to eating a lot of rubber chickens. Over and above the forty hours of work I put in during the week, I also must attend industry meetings if I want to continue building a clientele.

"If you chair a fund-raiser, not only do you come before all the members of that organization, but you also have the chance to earn credibility. It becomes a very strong recommendation without having to sell yourself. You are automatically presumed trustworthy."

Sharon's company has little competition in the marketplace.

"People just do not know how to do what we can do. In the last six years we have tripled our market."

When I interviewed Joy Riggs, head of Employee Development Systems, she told me she did not have to look far to find a profitable niche in the marketplace to showcase her skills. Over a decade ago she left teaching and began to write and sell training courses to Fortune 500 companies.

"My biggest seller is the course Personal Effectiveness, which is really about my life skills—how I motivate myself, speak positive affirmations, how to listen, etc."

Companies such as Caterpillar, American Stock Exchange, Kraft, and Texaco all buy her courses. She developed her niche by first joining associations such as the American Training Society. Once she knew who her customers were, she called the companies and asked, "Who is your training decision maker?" Riggs says we better know our customer or the call is a waste.

In 1983 her niche, which was limited to companies in Houston, Texas, suffered a big downturn. At that time Joy was conducting her own seminars, and she knew she had to look somewhere else for business because, due to budgets, training seminars were among the first projects to be canceled.

"I used that opportunity to package one of my courses. I created a video. It was a leader's guide and enabled others to teach my course. I leveraged me."

Now Riggs has over fifteen video courses and accompanying educational materials that sell for $5,000 each. Her reorder business is as high as 70 percent and her customers last over ten years.

"Liberty Mutual was one of my early customers for the employee course. Now they start all their managers out on our communication skills course. We have the kind of curriculum that they trust."

Riggs's rise to market penetration was based on a cold call and a question: "What do you need?" Then she would listen. Once they trusted her, she would write a specific program for each particular company and then go in and teach the course.

When tough times hit, Joy had the selling power to create an even bigger niche. She convinced her customers that her courses were great, the instruction manual was clear, and it was not necessary to hire her personally to teach the course.

Barry Kaye doesn't discount any niche, including advertising, which many of his insurance industry peers discredit. He advertises on CNBC several times a day and in *Forbes* magazine, as well as circulating his own twenty-four-page magazine. His book *Die Rich and Tax Free* is given away like popcorn. All of these different avenues generate over 250 leads a day, which he in turn doles out to his agents all over the country.

"I'll be the first to tell the new agent that my way may not work in the average income market. We have an affluent client, and a reputation, but for a long time it was important to attend that cocktail party and meet those new prospects. Clubs are important to join. Those old customers are very loyal and many have become my friends. Now I am at a social level where it would be poor manners to prospect under such circumstances. When my wife and I are out together, I still get the yearning to prospect, but she makes me promise to keep my mouth shut."

CUT TO THE CHASE

Joy Riggs and I both share the same philosophy about working the niche: Cut to the chase and use down-to-earth language. She asked, "What do you need?" I asked, "What do you think?"

Direct questions take people off guard because they are so used to a long line of baloney. When a financial planner cold-calls my home at night and says, "Well, how was your day?" or "Do you like to play golf?" I want to say, "Just spit it out, and ask me to buy something."

I prefer the "What do you think?" question.

"Think of what?" says the listener.

"What do you think of my product or service?"

"We never heard of it."

"Well, it's a good thing I called. I'll send you some information to study before you dismiss any possibilities."

Barry Kaye says, "You ask common sense questions. 'Why would you want your children to pay $600,000 to the government when you die, when for a much smaller investment your insurance policy could pay the government and leave your kids millions?' I'm on the war path, so I ask very direct questions. This stems from strong beliefs."

Brenda Burke gets right to the point with past satisfied customers: "Will you help me grow my business?"

We'll hear more from strategic planner Joey Tamer in the negotiating chapter, but her cut-to-the-chase questions—"Are you the decision maker?" or "Do you have the funds for this project?" or "What budget have you set aside for determining your entry strategy?"—are no-nonsense qualifiers that set her straight fast. She hasn't got time to talk to secondhand informants considering the high demand for her specialized services, and the tight schedule she keeps.

INVENTING NICHES

Sometimes just knowing where the hot prospects are is not enough.

Jim McMahon figured if he wanted to capture the real estate and building industry, it was not going to be by passing out rate sheets in offices as his competition had been doing for years.

McMahon says, "I wanted to provide value-added services and information. I became a student of the lending business, and I decided I had to approach my prospects armed with knowledge. Then I made a plan to get in front of the top one hundred real estate agents in the area. I went to various breakfast meetings to find out who the agents were who were listing and selling all the properties."

Once he knew who the top one hundred were, he put together a personal letter and a copy of that particular agent's listings. Then next to each listing he broke down what it would take for a buyer to qualify for that property. This was not being done by loan officers at that time.

He knew the high-powered agents were busy, so he told them he would only take fifteen minutes of their valuable time. He assured them that after fifteen minutes they would know how to qualify prospects from a lender's point of view. It did not bother him when agents refused his invitation; he knew they must not be the real winners he wanted to help.

McMahon's first ninety days in his business teaches us that people will not do business unless they are offered something unique. Jim tells new people:

"It takes 60 percent of the fuel to get the space shuttle off the ground. Then it floats around space for a month using up the other 40 percent."

His unique way of establishing, maintaining, and reinforcing the value of his services earned him the confidence of his customers. His idea, to see everybody he could *before* they bought a home, was very different from any other loan officer's approach.

He convinced the real estate agents to let him prequalify all of their prospects. This made his real estate agents and builders look good to the end user, and he knew when they looked good, he looked good.

"Always being different was my strategy for attracting the right prospects. For example, I work with a lot of relocation clients. Early on I taught the agents to let me prequalify their prospects before they arrived in town. I created a standard introductory dialogue that went like this:

"'I'm Jim McMahon, a loan consultant with CTX Mortgage. Realtor Mary Harker asked me to call you. I provide a free service for all of Mary Harker's clients just to make sure they are comfortable with many of the standard procedures when moving to the Dallas area.'

"Then I would go into a two- or three-minute prequalification, telling them something new about the area that they did not know previously. I anchored my relationship with them before they arrived."

Jim frequently uses the word "resource" when talking to his clients. He not only sells them a loan, but virtually becomes an encyclopedia of information for the relocation prospect.

"I tell relocation prospects to spend forty or forty-five quality minutes with me, not only getting a quick loan quote, but learning about the advantages and disadvantages of both fixed and adjustable rate mortgages. I let them know that most relocation prospects are only going to be in their homes for three to five years, and yet they still come in and tell me they want a fixed rate mortgage."

He suggests they take a look at the adjustable rate product. If the buyer pays the adjustable rate mortgage as if it were a fixed rate every month, he or she will be adding $300 or $400 a month to the reduction of his or her principal payment. This kind of information establishes Jim as a resource from the very beginning of the relationship.

Judi Sheppard Missett experienced some rejection and used the negative information to create a niche.

"I noticed a lot of women were coming through my classes and not staying. I was teaching a very hard class."

Judi realized nobody in her studio was going to go on to Broadway, and the class was too hard. This is when she started asking herself important marketing questions:

"Who were my students? They were mothers who were coming to a dance class with their children in the mornings.

"What did my students need and want? They wanted to re-live the fun they had when they were younger and going to dance class or when they were cheerleaders in high school.

"I changed the way I was teaching. I began to teach in a studio that had no mirrors. I wanted them to follow me and I incorporated my jazz dance moves into the class, but I made it much more fun and easy to follow. They mirrored me like people do when they play follow the leader. I praised them and reinforced what they were doing every step of the way."

Dance can be a very critical activity. Many dance teachers constantly point out what the student is doing wrong. Professional dancers can turn the negatives into positives. Judi's customers, however, weren't professional dancers and didn't need or want such harsh criticism.

"I changed everything based on looking at the hard truth. In the process I created a mass market niche for selling my programs. In my first class I had fifteen people, in my second class I had thirty people, and by the third class sixty people showed up. That's when I knew I had finally hit on something."

She was their mirror and their cheerleader, and they didn't have to think. All they had to do was come and have fun. In return they received lots of praise and the benefit of a good workout.

Judi could have limited herself to becoming an excellent dance teacher in a small studio focusing solely on the local community of advanced dancers. But instead she focused on a much larger percentage of the population—the mass market of ordinary people who wanted to improve their lifestyle and get fit without trying to win a medal.

EXPANDING NICHES WITH PASSION, POWER, AND CONFIDENCE

Meet Ken Rohl of KWC, Inc., who began selling luxury bath fixtures—starting with one high-end $390 bathroom faucet—out of his garage in the early 1980s and has since moved up to CEO of his own $10 million company. He explains how he expanded his product line in order to increase his market share.

"About three years ago we realized that the consumer environment was a lot different than it had been in the eighties. In the past, conspicuous consumption was big, but now we were into the value-added age.

"I looked at my product line one day after talking to a couple who said they wanted the low-end Mercedes rather than the high-end of Volkswagen. They admitted that two or three years ago they would have been looking at the high-end Mercedes. 'Former big spenders,' they called themselves. But now they had three children and debt. So they asked me what I had available in the low-end. That's when I panicked.

"Understand we were talking bathroom faucets, not cars, but it's a great analogy. I realized I had a good Mercedes Benz 400 but not a 300, or a 190. I immediately got on the phone with my partners in Switzerland and told them my needs. I wanted a $190 faucet. I wanted a $300 faucet. I already had my $400 model.

"The next three months we got to work—same quality without all the bells and whistles of the $400 model. I took a lesson from Mercedes and said we must keep the brand. It would have been a mistake to introduce a best, or a good, or a better, in a different brand.

"We spent a year introducing those other choices. It opened a lot of doors that were starting to close. Suddenly I was selling to lower-end builders. I sold the products to a builder with a 113-home project because I had a B- and a C-grade faucet now. If I hadn't developed those choices, I would not have had a market. The other lesson: Recognize the importance of brand equity and build on it. Don't sabotage it."

When Jenny Craig came back from Australia to sell her weight loss plan, she knew what was unique in Australia was not necessarily unique in the United States.

"We realized we needed to differentiate ourselves from other weight loss companies, so we introduced frozen foods to dieters.

"Convenience had become important because the two-paycheck family was beginning to grow. It was the quality of our frozen foods and the convenience of the microwave oven that put us on the map in the U.S."

Meanwhile in another part of the country Judi Sheppard Missett was formulating a business plan with her ten newly trained instructors which later turned out to be the beginning of Jazzercise franchising.

She decided she would train five women who had been with her for the previous five years. These women were passionate about Jazzercise, saw how it had evolved, and had a dance background. Judi was an organized person and had handwritten in a notebook every bit of choreography that she had ever done.

She shared the routines with the five women, told them how she expected a class to be taught, and said she would test them before they went out to teach a class. Little did she know that she was pioneering certification in the fitness industry.

"They began teaching, and students were calling me up and complimenting me on the marvelous classes my new teachers were conducting. By the end of 1977 I had trained ten people, and six of those teachers are still with me today.

"More teachers signed up," Judi says. "Two of the women

were teaching in 29 Palms and the Yucca Valley. One woman's husband, a local high school teacher, lent the women the school's antiquated video camera so my choreography meetings could be videotaped and sent to them."

Home video recorders came out a year later. Judi and Jack went out and bought a couple of cameras and she began videotaping her routines in the backyard amid the dogs and cats. The videos were copied and sent to instructors who were beginning to move all over the country.

Some of the husbands of the Jazzercise instructors got transferred in the military, and the women wanted to continue to teach in their new state. Judi began sending them choreography on video, and by 1979 she was sending routines to teachers not only in the United States, but also in Europe, Brazil, and Japan. By 1981 over twelve hundred instructors around the world were getting video instruction and certification from Jazzercise, and the Missetts had over thirty video recorders in their living room.

From there came JMP Productions, Jack and Judi's own television production company, where Judi and outside clients could produce video and television presentations.

Jazzercise's new market became Judi's impassioned teachers, who took her fitness message to a wider audience. Her key to a bigger market share was asking her customers what they wanted that she hadn't yet provided.

We created a bigger market share at Danielle Kennedy Productions by going to our past customers and asking them what type of in-house video training we could provide for their companies. I surveyed owners for over five years and listened carefully to what they told me. Ultimately, my customers were the designers of the sixteen-tape video system that expanded my market.

My customers told me they preferred training that was broken down into modules, with only one topic on each video instead of two or three separate programs on one video. This way the program could stand alone and be used both as a sales meeting tool and part of a training series.

It's not a coincidence we go to our customers for help in designing our products. It makes the future sale that much easier. It's as if we custom make the product or cater the service to the customer's specifications and needs; the customer has a hand in the invention process. It's pretty hard for a customer to resist buying a product he or she helped design.

At SmartPractice Jim Rhode had two choices:

"I could double our business by finding ten new dentists to call on, or I could go back to the ten dentists we were currently serving and show them how, by increasing their lab services from $3,000 to $7,000 a month, they could do more with their existing patients."

He would rather take an existing client to lunch then go find a new dentist.

"The following month the dentist would call me and say, 'Last month you took me to lunch. This month I'm taking you to lunch because your idea has increased my business.'"

Jim Rhode will be the first to admit that his business was founded on teaching very basic, freshman business principles. For example, traditionally a patient would come into the dentist and say, "Hey, Doc, can you do something about this missing tooth?"

"Nowadays the dentist has been trained to say at a regular checkup, 'Mr. Patient, have you thought about doing something about that missing tooth before you end up having to fix your entire mouth?' It is now a common practice in the dental field to strongly recommend preventative work."

One of his latest products was developed from a visit with his daughter, also a dentist, at her office one afternoon.

"She told me she was having problems with her thumb. She, like all my dentists, wore an ambidextrous glove which was known to eventually cause discomfort from constant movement of the thumb. So SmartPractice put the thumb in the correct place on the glove. Then we introduced our own brand of synthetic rubber gloves for people allergic to latex."

One of the firm's latest successes is a product called Soft Paws, which fits over a cat's claws to prevent scratching. It is sold through veterinarians. A vet invented them and went to SmartPractice for marketing and distribution.

"By studying the needs of our market, we have created hundreds of products. We listen and we are proactive. It has led us to interesting places."

SmartPractice owns a printing company too. When the dentists needed greeting cards and postcards, Jim would go out and buy them. Then he realized in order to give better and faster service, he should print his own cards. So he went out and bought a simple printing press.

"Then we found someone to run it. After we got that mastered, we went out and bought a more complicated one. Now we have six or seven pieces of Heidelberg equipment, including full color presses, die cutters, etc. We are a full-service print shop."

In addition to the hundreds of products SmartPractice offered, Naomi Rhode had a gift for communicating. So in the early seventies she began to speak for free to various dental groups. She was a dental hygienist with a caring spirit, so her lectures—on how a dentist could become more people-oriented—came from total credibility.

Today she and Jim are considered the foremost authorities on the building of a dental practice, and have a very successful speaking business.

The Rhodes' philosophies are similar to loan legend Jim McMahon's. McMahon and the Rhodes teach us to become a resource with every prospect we encounter. McMahon used to close nine out of ten of the people he presented to, and now, seven years later, he finds he ends up getting that tenth prospect too.

"That tenth guy comes back too. If you add value, you are different, and if you do it honestly, your business niche will automatically expand. I treat the prospect who wants a $50,000 house loan the same as I treat the prospect who is buying a million dollar mansion.

"I had a good referral last year from a friend," said McMahon. "The man was already filling out an application with another lender, but he was having some difficulty with that institution. I did not go after the man's business, but a financial planner friend of mine kept bugging him to do business with me. I merely acted as a resource to the man, giving him some needed information."

The loan applicant would have easily switched lenders, but Jim encouraged him to take his advice, stick with the other lender, who could structure the loan exactly as McMahon recommended.

"The long and short of it is, the man is moving his medical practice to another part of our city. Now, three years later, he is coming to me to make the loan on his new million dollar home."

Another way McMahon expands his market with past customers is by instructing them to call him yearly to discuss various options they have with their loans. Paying off principal or refinancing should not be decided because of something they heard from a friend or read in the paper. By giving his customers instruction at the time of the sale, he has automatically expanded his future market. McMahon initiates calls to those who don't check in yearly, and reminds them of their changing options.

No company in the juvenile products industry is better at expanding business with existing customers than NoJo, Inc. In the late sixties housewife Shirley Pepys couldn't buy a padded liner to fit her baby's plastic infant seat, so she quilted one for herself.

Before long Shirley and her neighbor Sylvia Noble had Sylvia's mother sewing up infant seat covers by the dozens in her garage and giving them as gifts to all their friends. Then they got the idea to sell them. They took a few samples down to the Bullocks Department Store in Santa Ana, California.

"We practically begged the buyer to display our covers in the baby department for a few days to see how they would go over. Three days later the buyer called and wanted to know our retail number because she wanted to buy ten more. We didn't even know what a retail number was!"

Once the infant seat cover was on the market, they expanded into other covers and bedding products. Then in the early eighties, Pepys saw the interest in home decorating take hold, so NoJo brought high design and fashion into the nursery. They diversified into accessories. By 1986 Pepys was the company's sole owner and expanded the product lines through licensing, mass marketing, and entry into foreign markets.

Twenty-five years later NoJo is the nation's leading designer and manufacturer of fashionable infant bedding and accessories. All parents want their baby to come into the world and go home to a NoJo nursery. NoJo's tagline is "Only the best for baby." They manufacture comforters, sheets, pads, blankets, towels, table covers, bumper pads, changing covers and pads, car seat and carrier covers, lamps, mobiles, and wall decor.

"We filled a need in the marketplace from the beginning, and that is what selling is all about," says CEO Shirley Pepys. "I think my strong suit is keeping up with the changes in the marketplace. We've seen a major transition in this society—with parents having children later in life, in more affluent circumstances.

"Today's parents are so eager for information that it has changed the way we market our products. For every dollar we spend on advertising, we spend an equal amount producing instructional materials. As a businessperson I am impressed with this new generation of people who have a genuine parental interest and devotion to children."

NoJo continues to open new markets by emulating the style of the food or retail industries.

Pepys says, "We practice 'program selling.' Program selling

means keeping a category together in one section of the store and presenting the products spectacularly. For example, when you go into a supermarket and Procter and Gamble has a display of related products, you no longer have to run all over the store to find bath and toilet products.

"Liz Claiborne and Ralph Lauren began program selling a long time ago. They have created their own mini-store within the bigger department store. The customer can start out looking for a blouse or a shirt and end up with a complete ensemble. NoJo is now making that type of program selling available to parents.

"The parents walk in as if they are walking into a nursery. And we also provide instant decorating ideas. We help the parents imagine: This is what my child's room could look like. They come in looking for a comforter, but what if it matches the dust ruffle, the canopy, and the mobile? And look, moisturizing products."

Pepys is a perpetual student and observer of trends in lots of industries.

"The cosmetics people have taught us so much about the 'free gift with purchase' concept. You know when you walk up to a Lancome counter that if you want a free gift you are going to have to spend X number of dollars. Cosmetics is one of the most profitable industries in the world because it is market driven. We can all learn from their example."

Peter and Kathie Davis mastered the art of expansion too. Eleven years ago Peter quit his job as a tennis coach to go into business with his wife Kathie. Their original mission was to write a newsletter and sell subscriptions to aerobic instructors around the country in order to educate and provide service. The fitness industry was growing and hungry for information.

"We didn't even have a business plan or a long-term concept in the beginning," says Peter. "After we had about eight hundred to a thousand members (who took about six months to a year to recruit), we created a second product inspired by letters from subscribers. In their letters they voiced a need for liability insurance referrals and an arena where instructors could come together and share ideas."

Peter and Kathie quickly expanded their market share by heeding their subscribers' advice. They would soon helm their first conference.

"I can still remember when we went out to reserve the hotel for our first conference. The hotel manager asked us how many people we thought would come. We said five hundred to a thousand, and they laughed at us. They told Peter and I we would be lucky if we got two hundred."

The Davises promoted the conference in their newsletter, sent out one brochure, and ran some advertising in *Shape* magazine. Eight hundred people turned up for the first conference. From one small newsletter grew the fitness industry's biggest, most widely attended conference, a highly respected certification program, teacher training, a magazine publication, and many other educational materials.

Angel Martinez knows a little bit about expanding a niche too. Originally Reebok's customer was mostly the male athletic shoe buyer, but Martinez brought the aerobic shoe and the awareness of women's fitness needs to the open market.

"Reebok was ready to create fitness awareness among women. Women were not getting the voice they needed in fitness. Up until the seventies women's fitness was GAA—Girls' Athletic Associations. Aerobics showed up as a huge opportunity to invent products and services for this new vast market. For aerobics a woman had a leotard but no proper shoes, and poor instruction by teachers during a time when there was no aerobic certification."

Instead of strictly appealing to the competitive athlete, Martinez went about inventing a way women could identify with fitness. The "Classic" Reebok aerobic shoe was invented— very soft and lightweight, but with plenty of support. It became a best-seller, and that product only scratched the surface of the women's market share for Reebok.

And from my friend and world-class salesman Tom Hopkins

I've learned how to convert anyone off the street with passion, power, and confidence. My husband and I went golfing with him once, and I saw how the power of passion, and the "free gift" promotion, opened up a niche Tom was anxious to penetrate.

Tom called the golf course about one hour before our tee time. He asked the switchboard operator for the name of the golf director and the time he was expected to arrive.

When they connected, Tom said,

"Hi, Jack. My name is Tom Hopkins and I want to stop by with a free gift for you this morning before I tee off at your course around 10:30. I golf all over the world and have presented this gift to many pros like yourself. They all love it. Can I drop it off at 10:15?"

He agreed to see Tom.

I've known Tom over twenty-two years, and nothing has changed. He still gets hyper when he's selling. He reminds me of a seven-year-old kid on Christmas morning. I thought he was going to jump out of his five-foot-four body when he said, "I get to play golf, and pro shops finally start making some profits too. What a winner."

At the course Hopkins marched up to the pro and said, "Hi, Jack, I'm Tom Hopkins. We spoke about thirty minutes ago. I have a gift for you. Can I take it into your office?"

Inside of a big box was his complete sales training library on twelve audiotapes, including workbooks. I overheard every word he said to the golf pro.

"Jack, I'm Tom Hopkins and I'm in the teaching profession just like you. I do not give golf lessons—I give selling lessons. I travel all over the world and play golf in between my speaking engagements.

"Because my whole life is about selling, I always watch to see how people sell to others. This is instinctive to me just like observing a golfer's style is instinctive to you.

"I must admit that I have never been to a pro shop where the staff is interested in selling their products to the public—a public that includes many professionals with the money to purchase what you sell. Do you have any idea how much this company could increase its profits if some sales efforts were made in your pro shop?"

Jack agreed and mentioned that the owners were always complaining that the pro shop never turned a profit.

"I want to make you a proposition. It costs $395 to send a salesperson to my boot camp in Arizona for three days, and that does not include airfare, hotel, and food. Those salespeople who attend turn company profits around once they've attended my program."

Tom then put his beautifully packaged materials on the desk and said, "This is the complete curriculum that I cover and it sells for $299, and it is yours free.

"All that I ask is for an invitation to play a free round of golf for myself, my wife, and our two friends today. Does that seem like a fair exchange?"

Jack was thrilled to grant the request. It seems his brother-in-law was a big Tom Hopkins fan, and he couldn't wait to call him up and say he'd met Hopkins in person.

COLLABORATION AND QUALITY

Collaboration can be handled two ways. First, two people of equal reputation from separate spheres of influence can come together to double their market penetration. Or secondly, an up-and-coming big-timer can team up with a proven winner. The benefits are obvious for the up-and-comer, but there may be some excellent advantages for the big-timer too.

Peter Davis says that relationships and collaborating with quality people were the two key factors that contributed to IDEA's early success.

"But none of those relationships would have been possible if Kathie and I did not create a quality product. We never thought of ourselves as salespeople. Neither of us had any kind of training in sales. What we always concentrated on, with the manufacturers and other sponsors who become involved in the events, was the product itself.

"It was our job to concentrate on making these events first-class. I felt if we did that, the sales aspect would just come naturally. And that theory of mine turned out to be true. Although no one knew who we were in the beginning, what we were doing was quality work, and important people wanted to be a part of that work."

They moved forward with great speed in the fitness industry by going out and getting experts to contribute articles to their newsletter.

"We decided in order to gain credibility in the marketplace we needed a kinesiologist, a cardiologist, a sports medicine representative, and a nutritionist."

The Davises talked to their friends, who gave certain recommendations, then they had to sell the concept and the newsletter to the experts. The advantages for the experts turned out to be many. As IDEA conventions grew and became the most important events to attend in the fitness industry, these experts delivered talks, sold their books and tapes, and increased their own notoriety.

Among the contributors to this book, the list of successful collaborations is unlimited. Dr. William Sears, a well-known pediatrician and his wife Martha, a registered nurse, developed "The Original Baby Sling." This is a nontraditional baby carrier, and it generated a new style of parenting called "Baby Wearing."

The sling holds the baby's body up against the parent, and its hammocklike design allows parents to "wear" their babies for long periods of time in comfort and without strain. With the baby's head supported and safely contained within the sling, the parent's hands and arms are free for other activities.

Dr. Sears and NoJo CEO Shirley Pepys joined forces, filling a need of today's parents for a closer bonding experience with their infants. NoJo manufactures the Baby Sling, and it was selected as "The Product of the Year" in 1989 in that industry.

Jewelry fashion designer Carolee Friedlander teamed up with Estee Lauder, creating a new and exciting way to wear makeup and jewelry. Customers like Bloomingdales and other top retailers jumped on their innovative in-store promotion suggestions called "Custom Color Consulations," offering women a complimentary Estee Lauder makeover by one of the company's expert makeup artists. The artist determines whether the person has "warm" or "cool" skin undertones, while a Carolee consultant coordinates a pearl ensemble to go with her new cosmetic shades.

After Evelyn Echols landed the Pepsi account, Joan Crawford and Al Steele became her newfound collaborators.

"Because I got them booked on the cruise ship, they told everybody they knew that I could do anything. Joan Crawford became my friend and sold me marvelously. Yes, she was a perfectionist and very demanding, but when you did a good job, she admired that and would go to the ends of the earth to help you."

The next call Evelyn got was from NBC. They were in charge of the arrangements for the Grace Kelly wedding, and they wanted Evelyn to go to Philadelphia to book all the guests' reservations to Monaco. This was a very difficult job because the guests kept changing their minds about how they wanted to get there. But, as always, Evelyn did an impeccable job, while NBC was watching her every move.

Soon NBC started giving her their travel arrangements, a couple executives at a time, but eventually she won over General Sarnoff, the chairman of the board, which landed her the entire NBC account. NBC referred her to RCA, and the impressive list of clients continued to grow. Because of one single mentor collaboration that came about from doing a quality job, Evelyn Echols moved quickly into the big time.

Naomi Rhode's speaking career in the dental industry was a perfect way to collaborate with her husband Jim.

"When Naomi started getting asked to speak all over the

country, she would answer, 'We would love to come.' It became a marriage defense council," says Jim.

The Rewards of the Payback Philosophy

It almost sounds sacrilegious to put words like image building and philanthropic in the same sentence, but with the legends their philanthropic endeavors automatically enhance their image. It just happens, kind of like the sale just happens. Nobody is giving to receive but that is how it works out.

"My biggest joy in life is giving away 50 percent of everything I make. But I can't give it away fast enough, because giving it away keeps piles more of it coming back. I'm not bragging. I am humbled that life has put me in such a position," says Joe Gandolfo.

Judi Sheppard Missett was able to express her sentiments and the sentiments of many of us when she commented about what she calls "giving back."

"I feel so lucky. What's happened to me could have happened to lots of people with a passion for what they do. I never forget that, and it's why I want to blend my business with giving back whenever I can.

"Maybe it's the old midwestern ethic that I was raised with—you only get what you work hard for, and if you have been blessed, you must return some of those blessings. But I believe that if you are just a taker, eventually you are going to take until there is nothing left."

Once Jazzercise made it to the big time, Judi was constantly coming up with give-back programs for various communities around the country such as those with cerebral palsy, or the American Heart Association, for whom she pioneered "Dance for Heart."

"The first show we did for cerebral palsy was in Cleveland,

Ohio. I remember myself and another instructor driving to the facility and wondering if anyone would show up. As we got closer, we noticed all these cars, and we commented to each other that we wondered what else was going on that day in Cleveland.

"Twelve hundred people came to participate. It was not our intention to do anything but give, and we got so much more back than we gave."

Jazzercise continues to break new ground because of the high-minded thinking of its founder. A few years ago the Kids Get Fit Program was instituted at Jazzercise locations around the country.

"Reports of how unfit today's children are is what motivated myself and the other instructors to do something about this around the country. Plus the future of Jazzercise depends on the kids of today growing up and seeking out ways to live a healthier lifestyle. Kids Get Fit reached ninety-five thousand children the first year, and as of this date over one million kids are participating."

One night in Chicago, at the height of her career as a travel agent, Evelyn Echols and her husband were having dinner with some judges from the local family court. They were telling Evelyn and her husband how impossible it is to educate children in reformatories.

"I said I presume that is true because, first of all, these kids are dropouts, secondly the teachers in reform school are duller than dishwater, and lastly no one is giving these children inspiration to seek a better life. Who could get excited about working at a fast-food restaurant when they got out? After all they could make more money stealing off the streets."

Evelyn told the judges she could teach the kids the travel business because it had a "dream quality."

"It says to them if you do this well, you can travel around the world, going places and doing things you never thought you would experience in your whole life."

She was asked to go out to the reform school and teach the

kids just that. She agreed, and then forgot about it. About three weeks later she received a telephone call from one of the judges, telling her they were ready for her course.

"I almost fainted. The reform school was for first-time offenders. No matter what age they were, they had to stay until they were eighteen, and graduated from high school. So I went out and interviewed the group that said they wanted to take the travel course. This crowd gave me the roughest time on earth."

Evelyn was challenged by one girl in particular. She was smoking a cigarette and wearing a chip on her shoulder the first time she came up to Evelyn.

"So you are going to teach me the travel business, huh?"

Evelyn responded dryly, "I don't think I could teach you anything."

Replied the girl:

"But I could teach you a few things. Do you know how to fly from Chicago, to New York, to Los Angeles, to San Francisco, and back to Chicago with five cents in your pocket?"

"No," said Evelyn.

Then the girl told Evelyn to sit down because she had done exactly that and now she was going to teach Evelyn the travel business.

The girl proved disruptive throughout most of the course. Finally Evelyn said to her one night,

"You are a leader in this class, and if you quit so will the rest of them. So I am going to do whatever it takes, even if I have to stay here until midnight with you, but you are going to graduate."

She told Evelyn she hated do-gooders.

"I could care less. If you don't finish this course, it'll be over my dead body," retorted tough-as-nails Echols.

From that night on the girl started handing in exceptional work.

"We began to build a relationship. She was a very attractive girl, except for a terrible nose. So I asked her what she thought about me arranging to have her nose fixed prior to graduation."

This gesture of generosity shocked her because she had spent her whole life either having her nose broken by people, or getting teased unmercifully about it. So with the girl's enthusiastic response, Evelyn called a top plastic surgeon and scheduled the surgery. He did a first-class job and Evelyn's toughest student was on cloud nine.

"I decided I wanted to do something exciting for the entire graduation class—something that would help them understand what potential they now possessed because they had put themselves through the rigors of this course."

She went out to United Airlines and asked the vice president to give her an airplane because she wanted to take the kids up in the air for graduation, serve them lunch, and pass out their diplomas. After a lot of coaxing United agreed.

"Then I called on Marshall Fields because the graduates needed new outfits. We had their hair done, the whole works. When we arrived at the airport the day of the graduation, we saw that United had contacted the press. *Time* magazine, *Newsweek*, Associated Press, NBC—they were all on board when we took off."

The following week, back at her office, Evelyn's phone was ringing off the hook. People from all over the United States wanted to know how they could sign up for her travel school.

"We told them that unless they were incarcerated or in reform school we could not help them."

An evening with the judges opened up a brand-new market for Evelyn Echols—a market that would eventually make her a legend in the hotel and travel training world. Based on the response of the publicity, Evelyn realized there was a big need in this country for a first-class travel and hotel school. Europe was the only place travel and hotel people could get first-class training.

She decided to run a test ad to see if there were any

prospects in the marketplace. She had no program formulated, and no brochures. Eight hundred people responded to her first ad.

"I flew back to New York and called on all the carriers I was involved with and said I wanted to form the first travel school in the United States provided they would serve on my board of directors; they would endorse it; they would agree to teach at the school."

Echols got full agreement, flew back home, and put together a quality program, but a "very crappy brochure." One month later the Echols International Hotel School was up and running, with fifteen students enrolled. Today it has been voted the best travel school in the United States.

John and Donna Crean built an entire estate complex with the sole purpose of sharing their home with good causes in the southern California area—a large space for fund-raisers or events. On Super Bowl Sunday hundreds of people come to the Creans' and enjoy a fund-raiser Super Bowl party. In the middle of the summer there may be a circus in the Creans' backyard, with profits going to the Dance Outreach charity for handicapped children.

On the first floor of "Village Crean" is a modest twelve-hundred-square-foot apartment where John and Donna live. They never use the rest of the home, except when the guests arrive.

"This place would be dismal for just two people. We are thrilled to open our home. It wouldn't be any fun around here without all the goings-on. We are all just renting the earth anyway."

Another earthly tenant, Barry Kaye, says, "We have a God-given ability. We receive a lot of luck to make things happen, and I believe we have an obligation to pay back society for these fortunate circumstances."

The list of his paybacks are endless. Most recently the Carole and Barry Kaye Museum of Miniatures, the largest contemporary museum of miniature furniture in the world, located in Los Angeles, hosted a fund-raiser with Elizabeth Taylor and raised lots of money for AIDS.

Some critics claim they do it for image, or market share, or other self-serving motives. But for the Creans, Judi Missett, Evelyn Echols, Joe Gandolfo, and Barry Kaye the rewards are much more far reaching.

Chapter Three Review

- The entire population is your market.
- Do not presume the worst prematurely.
- Rejection is part of the game.
- Prospect, then leave the rest in God's hands.
- Do not cut off opportunities and eliminate niches.
- Be bold and courageous and go door knocking.
- Call on past customers. It's the quickest way to build goodwill and turn a profit.
- Volunteer in your industry as a gesture of gratitude.
- Know your prospect before you make the call.
- Cut to the chase and use down-to-earth language.
- Know more than just who and where your hot prospects are.
- Become a student of the market you wish to penetrate.
- Be a resource of knowledge to your customers.
- Ask your customers what they want, then give it to them.
- Listen more.
- Expand your business with existing customers.
- Keep up with the changes in the marketplace.
- Present your products spectacularly.
- Be a perpetual student.

- Partner with someone of equal reputation from another sphere of influence.
- Return the blessings.

THE WARM-UP THAT ELIMINATES THE UNWORTHY COMPETITION

"Getting ready is the secret of success."

—HENRY FORD

DAILY BUSINESS development became a routine for me, and in the course of the activity I learned to enjoy thoroughly the interaction with the public. I have come to find out just how true my Irish grandfather's advice was. He passed it down to us grandkids in the form of a poem:

Smile and the world smiles with you.
Weep and you weep alone.
For the cheerful grin,
Will get you in,
Where the kicker is never known.

His advice, along with having a super salesman for a father, and being raised in the friendliest of environments, contributed to my personal sales success. I grew up in the 1950s, on the west side of Chicago, with the Italians, the Irish, and the Greeks. These people could start a conversation with anyone. Either they knew you, thought they knew you, or knew someone who did know you.

"Aren't you related to Ruth O'Leary's niece?"

"No, but my second cousin is."

"I thought so. I went to school with your mother's sister Ann. You resemble that side of the family."

My father, Joe Barrett, loved playing off such conversations. He was one of those people whom everybody felt comfortable talking to, because he loved all forms of humanity. On Saturday he and I walked down to Jack's ice cream parlor. It was only four blocks away, but sometimes it took hours to get there because Dad had a question or a comment for every other person who passed by. To the boy at the newsstand he would say, "Sell a million of 'em, Johnny. Someday you're gonna own this corner."

As the local police officer would drive by, Dad would yell, "Top of the morning to you, Captain Larry O'Sullivan. Did you catch any bad guys today?"

Once we got to the ice cream place, it was another two hours of yapping. Dad wanted to know about everybody, how they were doing, and most of all he was looking for a good story. I remember saying to him once, "Dad, everywhere we go people seem to know you."

Then he passed on the best advice I have ever received about warming up contacts.

"Honey, never forget as you go through life that there really are no strangers out there. We all have so much in common with each other. We all need to go to the bathroom several times a day. All of us want to make enough money to pay off all of our bills, and still have plenty left over at the end of the month to save or go out and spend on some fun.

"Everyone wants to be a good parent too. We all love to get

a raise, and most certainly we love praise. And most of all we all want to live to a ripe old age, and die quietly in our sleep."

I named Dad's attitude "The Walk-in-Like-You-Own-the-Place Mind-Set." I have never forgotten what he told me and have applied his wisdom to all I serve.

Warming up the prospects before a brilliant presentation starts with the mind-set—the mind-set of a lover of people, of a friend who cares about the other's best interest first, of a salesperson who possesses a strong conviction that he or she is on a mission.

Lane Nemeth possesses the mind-set and the mission.

"All the problems of the world boil down to a lack of self-esteem," says Discovery Toy's first lady. "So everything we create and develop at Discovery Toys is based on building up the child's sense of greatness and wonder. I have never considered myself a toymaker, but rather an esteem builder. It's my lifetime mission. It's the mind-set I wake up with every morning and go to bed with every night. It generates so much excitement in my world."

CREATE EXCITEMENT

Money can't buy excitement. Excitement is generated from inside our heart and soul, and spreads outward, projecting our certainty to the client. It must be present during the warm-up phase. During recessionary periods in our economy, it is very difficult to create initial excitement because the prospect is not as trusting, but for pros like Evelyn Echols, the warm-up becomes an opportunity to generate excitement.

"During big layoffs in the travel industry Echols Travel Schools warm up prospective students by conducting free seminars, and showing them that despite layoffs, we are able to place 94 percent of our students."

Evelyn, like Shirley Pepys and Tom Hopkins, says the word "free" is a powerful way to create excitement during the approach stages. Free gifts, free seminars, free consultations. Seminars create excitement because they bring lots of people together with a common interest in a product, service, or field. Where two or more interested parties are gathered together, the chances of creating excitement improve.

Echols has an innate ability to create her own excitement.

"When my travel agency was booming, I remember walking down a street in New York one day and running into the owner of the third largest television station in the area. He asked me to do a travel television show for his station."

It didn't matter that she had never done a TV show in her life.

"I started doing one half-hour show a day and interviewing VIPs such as U.N. delegates. The show went over so well, I ended up with six half-hour shows a week for two years. All of this brought in business."

Holding travel seminars opened up other opportunities for Evelyn Echols. One day a woman came up to her at the end of the program and introduced herself as the owner of *Holiday* magazine. She wanted Evelyn to be the bureau chief for the midwest. Once again Evelyn admitted she knew nothing about doing a column in a magazine, but she'd give it a try.

Evelyn's excitement about her work, and her willingness to try new promotions for the sake of her work, woke people up to the virtues of her business.

Judi Missett did the same thing when she tried her hand at writing Jazzercise press releases to generate excitement.

From an early age Fred Segal created excitement with his customers by using his heart more than his head.

"Friendship and family mean everything. I grew up in a dysfunctional family with an absentee father and a mother who was hardly there. I don't think I realized this at first, but I created excitement in my stores out of my need to connect. My store became a meeting place for people to come and feel good. We even had music in the store so people could dance while they were shopping."

Angel Martinez created a similar synergy in his first business.

"My customers weren't there to buy shoes. Those types of customers went to a department store. The clientele I attracted heard we had something more to offer—another way of life that started with running. Customers would come in and talk for hours about marathons, better times, newest shoe styles, and energy food for runners. Of course we sold lots of running shoes, but something else was happening. An excitement was present in the air. A whole new fitness culture was growing."

THE SECRET POWER OF PREPARATION

Rumor has it in Hollywood that Robert DeNiro is one of the most prepared actors of our time. On the first day of shooting for a film, DeNiro needs no script. His lines have been mastered. While the rest of the cast fumble through scripts for the first several days, DeNiro begins traveling inward to attach to his character's personality and essence.

Performance presentations are not spontaneous events. When the famed courtroom attorney nicknamed Racehorse Haynes was interviewed by *Texas Monthly* years ago and asked how he won cases, he claimed "I am not smarter than other attorneys. I am just better researched and better prepared."

Josie Natori repeatedly mentions her experience as a concert pianist in the same conversation with a discussion of selling.

"Practice and preparation are everything. I worked at the piano sometimes eight hours a day. I think this type of discipline and preparation gave me advantages when I got into business. I had enough discipline to study intently, and I took this discipline to Wall Street when I got out of school, and later when I changed careers and moved into the lingerie business.

"I knew nothing about either of these businesses when I began, but it was my willingness to study and prepare that gave me the advantage of being confident when I went out on presentations."

Ice skating taught me how to discipline myself at an early age. From the ages of eight to fourteen I spent most mornings between 5 A.M. and 8 A.M. on the ice. Although I never made it to the Olympics, the discipline that I developed during those early morning hours has served me well as an adult in sales."

Preparing is risk taking. Jewelry maker Carolee's willingness to prepare led her to France in the early days of her jewelry business. There she found the components and pieces that were not commonly used in this country in jewelry making.

"Differentiation demands preparation," she says. "Part of that preparation is studying other competitors, and then deciding what you can present in the future that no one else is offering."

At Discovery Toys a great deal of time, money, and research has been spent on child development.

"More and more we are understanding that children see and respond more than we ever imagined. This whole notion of just giving the baby a black-and-white toy for three months is nonsense. Now the timing is down to six weeks. So I am not going to have a whole line of products for babies up until three months that are only in black and white," says Lane Nemeth.

Part of Discovery Toys' preparation is going out into the marketplace and testing products on kids.

"This is how we found out that kids were sensitive to scents. We developed a line of products based on this information. We have huge organizations that provide us with the latest findings about what children are responding to positively. Presenting the finished product is so much easier when you start by doing your homework."

"Don't forget, a well-prepared salesperson is an experienced salesperson," says SmartPractice President Jim Rhode.

"I know that I speak with much more power and confidence than I did fifteen years ago, because I have been through it. I find that hard-won experience and the confidence that I bring to the presentation has an important side effect: I no longer have to please people. I can speak from the heart and give people my wealth of knowledge, and be at peace knowing I speak from a rich knowledge base."

Scientist turned super saleswoman Dr. Sharon D'Orsie of Eagle Environmental gained a large foreign chemical company with a U.S. facility as a client because of her thorough preparation. They were facing allegations of wrongdoing in their safety and health programs, so they were looking for a company to do a very comprehensive safety and health audit.

Because of the scrutiny connected with this company, it was a highly visible job. Sharon recalls, "There were three pieces to the puzzle. We put them together, outperformed the competition, and closed the sale."

She says she closed the deal because of three reasons: (1) Her company had technical expertise. But Sharon is quick to mention that a lot of firms had technical knowledge, so knowledge by itself was not responsible for the sale. (2) She did her homework, and focused on results. (3) Her company's code of ethics.

"We have a written code of ethics which is periodically reviewed. The fact that the client was facing allegations of wrongdoing, and the fact that I mentioned in passing that we did business consistent with the highest ethics of our profession, really sealed the deal.

"In anticipation of the final sales meeting, I went to Rice University library and acquired a book from the Harvard University School of Asian Studies that talked about doing business in this particular foreign country. I learned everything I could about the country of origin before I made the sales presentation."

Sharon warmed her prospects up by emphasizing the knowledge she had, her reputation, and her ethical standards. But the thing that cinched the sale was her preparation, the time she took well in advance to listen to the customer.

Salesman and CEO John Marconi of Orange Coast Title in southern California credits "strictly preparation" for his dramatic sales success in his early years in the title business.

"For the first year and a half I was in the title plant searching for titles. Actually, I was down there compiling records. Because of that period of preparation, I still know the title business very well. I was the youngest title officer out west in the sixties. Prior to turning twenty-one years old I was given a title unit. So there I sat with a series of customers and a territory."

Marconi said most title sales reps were public relations people in those days. A handsome young man would call on a young and beautiful escrow officer, invite her to lunch, and get the title order based on the "restaurant choice and how smooth of a talker he was."

"If complex questions about title reports, signatures on deeds or liens came up, the rep replied with a 'Hey baby, don't worry about it. When I get back to the office, I'll have the guy check it out and then call you back.'

"But what made me unique was that I was that guy back at the office too. My strong selling point was that I was going to handle everything. The same guy who was out on the street pitching for the title order was going to go back to the office to handle the problems. No middle man. Just me—eyeball to eyeball with the customer all the way through the deal. It was a very unique role during that period of time in the title business."

Marconi, an east coast transplant, says he was raised with a strong work ethic.

"I was taught that you earn your pay—versus you have the right to it because you showed up. It was easy for me to become number one. Most of my competition just showed up and put a lot of emphasis on looking the part."

Marconi remembers taking home at least twenty-five files a night and working on them. Preparation and going the distance is only half of his success formula.

"You have to dramatically point out to the customer that what you are doing for them is brilliant. If you treat all this extra service as mediocre, that is exactly what the customer is going to think it is."

Prepare, but get the points. Do not prepare meticulously and then figure everybody is happy. Do not assume that the customer knows you extended yourself.

"You aren't cocky when you talk to the customer about all the work you have put in to please him or her," says John. "You just make a phone call and let the customer know he or she does not have to worry because you got ahold of the attorney.

"You convinced the attorney to sign the papers three hours earlier. You, personally, drove the documents to the bank, which was sixty miles away from your office. Salespeople do not go for that extra squeeze with the customer. And yet that extra service, when pointed out, is the very thing that brings the salesperson future repeat business."

David Steitz believes in "preparation before the fact." He began his business and built his first customer base by doing a market study with prospective users.

"I called prospects and said, 'Hi, I'm David Steitz and I am putting together a business plan to set up a computer typesetting company. If there were a new service for this, what kind of things would it have to offer? What would you be interested in? What would you try?' "

He was able to take that information, some sound dollar estimates of what the market was like, and his knowledge of the competition to begin a business. Calling on customers with such credible preparation under his belt put his new company in the forefront twice as fast as most start-up businesses. Steitz still uses the customer market study.

"We just finished preparing to set up a new division for short-run color printing in the exact same way. We called our customers. We are the second installation for this technology in the United States. It is so new that we are having to explain to people what it is and how to use it."

Steitz considers himself a measured risk taker because he does not take a fly-by-the-seat-of-his-pants approach to what customers want and how he is going to sell his products to them. Characters, Inc., frequently uses questionnaires and focus groups to prepare themselves for objections that they may hear in the marketplace.

"We will get a group of three to eight of our customers together over breakfast, lunch, or dinner and give everyone a chance to speak. We ask them how well our company is meeting their present needs. This gives us ideas for change and improvement. Then we ask them what their future needs are, or what we could be offering that they are not getting now.

"Our company has grown from typesetting to desktop publishing to color separations, and recently to presentation graphics, video editing, and slides. For this growth we are much in debt to our past and future customers."

Shirley Pepys says that the standing joke in the corporate office at NoJo is "When all else fails, go out and ask the customer.

"So many of the giant companies have gone through the same realization after they sit around pondering and brainstorming and proposing unrealistic marketing efforts.

"NoJo has a company store adjacent to corporate headquarters, and those customers who walk in off the street form a large part of our focus groups.

"We leave a sign-up sheet at the location and invite people

to join our advisory group. We indicate when the next meeting will be and offer a gift cetificate.

"Of course our customers are moms and we get the real scoop from them and the grandmothers, as well. The meeting takes about two hours and is probably the most enlightening two hours of my day."

Pepys sits in the back of the room and does not identify herself as the owner.

"I have so much fun, and if they knew I was the owner, all of that would end."

The NoJo team stays on the cutting edge because of the invaluable feedback they get from these parents.

"Parenting has changed dramatically. Today's parents are educated parents, and educated parents means product."

Since 1990 Palmer Homes of Austin, Texas, has gone from a small two-man development company to one of the top fifteen building companies. This is because the owners—Bill Palmer and Doug Clark—prepared their product and sales presentations with the help of those they serve.

"We went to the local real estate agents and asked them how they could help us sell our new homes. They told us how they wanted to be compensated and treated, and we met their requests. We pay excellent commissions to resale salespeople who bring customers into our models, as well as paying our on-site people commissions too."

The Palmer group allows customers to select floor plans from dozens of different home designs, or to customize their own plan. They made this option available after conducting extensive market research that told them today's consumers wanted more control of what they were buying and that they were extremely value-driven.

Angel Martinez of Reebok was a cross-country runner in high school and college. When he opened Island City Sports in the Bay area, he was an avid student of fitness. When customers dropped in, they knew he was a resource of information, and in essence they were buying his knowledge as well as his shoes. His warm-up approach, which couldn't help impressing the customer, began with his extensive knowledge of running and led to the healthy benefits that resulted.

In Maryles Casto's first year in her travel business, it was her willingness to research her clients' needs that quickly put her into the big time. In her warm-up with the top executives she proved that if she got a crack at their business, she could guarantee no-questions-asked, first-class service.

"These executives don't want to hear they can't get on a flight, or can't sit by the window in bulkhead in first class. They hate the word 'can't,' and I knew if I used that word the first time out with these folks, I would never get their business back."

She found a way to build a mistake-proof system for service.

"I zeroed in on the secretaries at these companies who were doing the reservations. I figured if they knew what went on behind the scenes we could all get the details handled more efficiently—details like what flights were most desirable, what seat assignments were important to their bosses, etc. I wanted to put these secretaries in my shoes, and make them look like heroes to their bosses."

So on the weekends Maryles rented a bus and took groups of secretaries out to the airport to show them how check-ins were done, how meals were prepared. At the time no one in the travel business was doing these demonstrations. The education showed them that they did not have to take no for an answer when their bosses had special requests.

She told the secretaries that both they and their bosses were not her clients, but her guests. Her job was to make them feel welcome. Warming up the secretaries by sharing her knowledge about the travel business helped Maryles create inroads with companies like Intel and Apple during her first year as an entrepreneur.

In the speaking business, researching the audience is the key to instant rapport building. When I did the Tupperware Starfest Shows around the country, I went way back into the history of Earl Tupper and collected some relics, including Tupperware from my grandmother's collection.

When I walked on stage with one of her original Tupperware pieces, telling them how it had been passed on to me with love, the crowd went wild. Before the speech I went to Tupperware parties, and talked to staff at the home office, learning the vernacular of the company and other tidbits, such as never to call the cover of a Tupperware container a "lid," but to call it instead a "seal." Not knowing small details like this during the warm-up can kill the presentation.

My friend John Crean used his own customers and dealers as a valuable research source.

"When I first started in the business, I built a trailer product that I thought was pretty hot. I took it around to the dealers to see what they thought about it. Some of them were lukewarm on the thing, but because I was young and ambitious and could put the hustle on them pretty good, they ordered one anyway.

"I got it into production, but nothing much was happening with it. I needed more orders to produce more, so I got in my car, and when I hit the first dealer, he was very honest with me. He said 'This is a piece of you-know-what. What are you trying to put on me here?'

"I was still a very new guy on the block, but I did something right. I asked him why he didn't think he could sell it. Then I asked him what he thought would sell."

He took John out into the lot and showed him a used trailer that consistently sold within two or three days after it was put out there. John said it was a model that had been out of production since after the war, but was fairly functional.

"So instead of going on the rest of my trip to hunt down more orders, I went back to my motel and spent the night designing a different product, based on the little trailer the dealer had shown me. Then I went back to the shop, and told the guys to stop production on the one we were doing."

John said that when he sold venetian blinds, he knew it was a good product; everybody knew it was a good product and there was no hustle necessary to sell them. The enthusiasm was there. But he found out the importance of knowing your customer when he tried to push a trailer product down his dealer's throats.

"When there is no enthusiasm, research a customer and then go back to the drawing board and invent what they want. Until this day, if I don't see enthusiasm and excitement coming from those dealers, I know I am dead in the water," says Crean.

My old friend sales trainer Dave Grant suggests making regular warm calls to past customers to say hi without asking for anything.

I find it a good time to do some research and ask them for suggestions on ways to improve what I sell. The side benefit? Opportunities to research past customers become business development opportunities too. I've received some wonderful improvement-of-service ideas from my clientele, with a valuable P.S. — "By the way I have a prospect for you. Remind me to give you the name and number before you leave."

DIFFERENTIATION

There is nothing that endears us to the customer faster than being truly unique and different, along with the promise of good service. Then the customer knows from the onset we are not going to be wasting his or her time. Jenny Craig was only able to break into the U.S. market when she differentiated her programs from others through the introduction of quality frozen foods.

Fred Segal differentiated with fashion jeans.

Angel Martinez with aerobic shoes for women.

This critical principle must be applied every time we pick up the phone, or send out a letter, brochure, press release, or mass mailers.

It took Dynacom's Allan Gibby two months to get his first sale, which wasn't bad considering he generated that sale through a mass mailer. He had no video equipment, but what he knew for sure was that he wanted to do sports production. He was prepared to produce corporate videos or any other type of production just to get rolling, but he targeted his passion toward the sports market first.

He connected in the warm-up because he differentiated himself by being refreshingly honest and innovative.

"I sent out the mailer to all the ski resorts in the country, and then I went up to television stations in Los Angeles and told them I wanted to get a show on the air called 'Skiers Update.' I got one of the new, smaller stations to sell me a half hour. Then I got a response off the flyer from the ski resort in Taos, New Mexico, saying they wanted to do a show with me."

Gibby's last $170 took him to New Mexico and he sold the show off his vision.

"When I went into that first presentation and sat in front of those executives, I was petrified. They knew I was afraid, but I figured I was just going to be Allan Gibby, and not build up some scenario that was bigger than I really was. I told them my idea, explained what I could do, and was very honest about it."

Gibby was different in two ways: He wasn't playing the role of hype pitchman, and he came up with a new strategy of promotion by enticing skiers to a resort—via television informercials. His show aired on Christmas Day, showing all the resorts at the Taos Ski Valley and some really hot skiing. Until then no one in sports production had ever marketed that way.

"My brochure was plain old black and white. I had no money, so I even did the pasteup myself," says Gibby.

Being different took Hollywood agent Michael Ovitz out of the mail room at the famed William Morris Agency and into the big time. The head of the agency was impressed when he found Michael working at 11 P.M. one night going over the day's mail. Six months later he was made an agent. By 1975

Ovitz and four other agents had left the William Morris Agency and set up Creative Artists Agency.

The story goes that they started in a tiny rented office space, with some card tables and chairs, a couple of phones, and their wives helping with office duties. Business was slow at first, with only a handful of stars joining them. But once again Ovitz proved that being different pays.

He saw the power in Hollywood coming from good screen-writers and other producers of raw material. Good stories always lured the stars. So Ovitz contacted Morton Janklow, the powerful New York literary agent, and began his ride to the big time. *Business Week* magazine profiled Ovitz, and the following excerpt proves that different is always better:

"Packaging, a common notion these days, didn't exist in feature films when Ovitz began. But it was old hat in television and radio. Basically, a network planning a new show would turn to an agency such as William Morris to supply writers, actors, and a director. Ovitz wanted to do the same for movies, but he needed compelling material.

"So for a year Ovitz phoned Mort Janklow's office every Thursday morning at 10:30 sharp. 'You could set your watch by him,' recalls Janklow. 'Finally I gave him a project that had fallen apart.'

"Within weeks, Ovitz had lined up Charlton Heston and Billy Dee Williams for the project, a story about a small-town police force called *Chiefs*. Better yet, CAA sold it to CBS, Inc., for three times what Janklow says he expected to get. An informal partnership was born that gave CAA access to hundreds of Janklow's stories. Among them: Thomas Harris's *Silence of the Lambs*."

This turned out to be only one example of differentiation for Ovitz. *Business Week* calls his company's relationship with Coke, "a case study of his methods." He proved over time to Coke that CAA could produce commercials as well as any ad agency. Ovitz hired Len Fink, one of the top creative guys at Chiat/Day, Inc., to teach CAA the ad business.

I find in my speaking business that the client is no longer satisfied to call my office, get a fee, size up comparable speakers, compare my video demo and brochures to other speakers, and then make a decision.

Instead the client is requiring that each finalist they are considering for the job must submit an outline or proposal.

What can I teach them?

What experience do I bring to the table? By experience they mean specifically what do I know about their business that they don't, that they need to find out to improve their bottom line?

I created my "Get Real" motivation presentation because I heard clients say to me, "We want to be entertained and educated." Thus the concept of "edu-tainment"—which was originated in the schools to find more interesting ways to hold children's attention when adults taught them about anything from good nutrition to drug abuse.

My goal is that "Get Real," an autobiographical tale communicated through speech, song, dance, and multimedia, will be the way the convention people differentiate me from other speakers in the nineties. I must take this differentiation factor into consideration when the copy is being written for the brochure, during creation of the video, and especially while drafting all personalized letters to meeting planners, who receive hundreds of solicitations a day.

One of the best ways to differentiate myself in sales is by emphasizing the extent of my experience. There is no substitute for experience, and I have it, so I play it up big. There is nothing any salesperson in an audience can throw at me that I will not be able to resolve. I don't care if it is insurance, real estate, cosmetics, or computers; I know customers inside out, and my audiences cannot be bluffed. I have the content and the sensitivity for one reason and one reason alone—I did it. I walked the talk. I sold in the trenches. My experience level always has and always will differentiate my work.

SERVICE MEANS SERVILE

Evelyn Echols says that America does not understand that real service means being servile.

"When you have a servile attitude from the get go, it is going to be hard for the customer not to warm up to you real fast. How can they resist doing business with you if you are such a refreshing change in the marketplace?"

I was fascinated by her use of the word "servile," because I saw some very important answers contained in that word. It means "having the spirit of a slave. Being subject to or obedient to whoever it is that you serve."

What might appear to be slavery to one individual is an act of service or love to someone else. When I was a new saleswoman I was criticized for "acting like a slave" because I offered free consulting services to homeowners. John Marconi says he acted very servile when he was the new kid on the block in the title business.

"Everybody, including myself, goes through about six months of just placating everybody. Not trying to take a stand on almost anything. It was 'Hey, whatever you want me to do, I'll roll over and do for you.' But it's an important time in any new salesperson's career."

The majority of your peers will criticize your subservience. "You are wasting your time with those losers."

"Go where the money is" seems to be the motto of those destined for eternal mediocrity.

Being servile has never been a strategy to me. I just wanted to prove I could help and be valuable, hoping that maybe prospects would be pleased with my willingness to serve, and spread good rumors about me to their friends. Maybe they would never buy from me, but I understood early on the power of their mouths as my advertising tool, not to mention the fact that I was getting actual experience while waiting for my market to open.

John Crean's hands-on servile style of doing business is the same now as it was when he was a struggling new salesman. Recently, he set his alarm for five o'clock in the morning because he had gotten word at four o'clock the previous afternoon that one of his new products, which had been shipped to Pennsylvania, had major window leaking problems. It was discovered during a bad rainstorm.

"It was a disaster. It was one of the suppliers that I had got started in business. I was out at the plant by 7 A.M. I found out that the manufacturer of the windows had had to have emergency surgery during the production time, so the shop was without supervision, leaving my windows shoddily built and prone to leaks."

John said when he got word of the problem, "It bugged me to no end. I couldn't sleep until I found out what happened. I explained to the customer that everything would be rectified."

Helen Gurley Brown's spirit of service and going the extra mile warmed up her first customer—her boss Don Belden— back in the days when she was a secretary at the ad agency Foote Cone Belding.

"All of us are selling every minute. I tried to please Don by writing entertaining and original letters. It wasn't long before he promoted me to copywriter."

In 1965 Helen became the editor in chief of *Cosmopolitan*. Since that time the magazine's sales and advertising revenue have risen spectacularly. *Cosmo* now sells just under 3 million copies and is one of the five largest-selling magazines on the U.S. newsstands. Helen says, "Once you figure out what you are good at, you go out and warm up your prospects by bending over backwards to please."

Today's consumers are value-driven and service-oriented. They are much more accountable for the buying decisions they make, and not dazzled by superlatives and phony sales talk, especially in the initial stages of the relationship. What impresses people is an attitude of gratitude that is intermingled with a quiet determination and superior knowledge of one's product. There is no shortcut to a better warm-up.

Speed and Fast Reaction Counts

We live in a fast-paced, rapid-service, microwave-oven, twenty-four-hour, ATM, Fax-it-to-me-now-baby society. If we want to really warm up our customers, we must show them how quickly we can react.

We all know that we accomplish more tasks in a day of crisis than in a month of complacency. The secret is to keep this sense of urgency alive. Two super salesmen built enormously successful enterprises based on speed. Tom Monaghan, founder of Domino's Pizza, made a fortune by building a company based on delivering hot pizza fast, and Fred Smith, who founded Federal Express Corporation, made one giving customers guaranteed overnight delivery service.

It seems like such an obvious habit of success, but speedy reactions are rare and continue to amaze our customers. Ken Rohl responded to a call at eight o'clock in the morning, five minutes after a builder called him complaining that he was having problems with one of Rohl's products.

"It turned out to be a competitor's product and not ours, but the builder was apologetic and went on for fifteen minutes about how impressed he was that I returned his call. He said it was just about impossible to reach a really responsible person when he had problems among any of his suppliers.

"Much of this lack of hands-on caring is gone because there have been so many mergers and takeovers, and the personalities of the original owners are no longer there. The commitment the owner built the business on has been lost. Nobody cares."

SmartPractice has increased their service substantially in

the last twenty-four months by same-day shipping on all orders, even if it is a print order.

Jim Rhode says, "To make this happen, we bought into technology, and shifted people's work schedules. For example, the people that imprint the cards used to come in at 6 A.M. and go home at 3 P.M. Now they come at 10 A.M. and go home at 7 P.M. Any job that comes to us before 5 P.M. goes out that same night."

Rhode says, "As recently as ten years ago it would take up to six days for an order to get through the plant, but now it takes less than four hours. Speed counts no matter what the circumstance.

"We used to handle a Christmas card order placed in September very differently too. We figured we had another month before we had to think about getting the order out. Now it goes out the same day, for the customer's sake but also to train us and keep us consistent."

Helen Gurley Brown thinks that phone calls aren't followed up, and business is not seized, because there are many people in the sales field that cannot deal with the freedom.

"You have to be a self-starter. Even if you work for a boss and he or she allocates the amount of time you need to put in for prospecting, it is up to the salesperson to go out there and do it. It takes self-discipline and gumption," says Helen.

When I went out on appointments, I used to call them auditions because the prospects who interviewed me were also interviewing two or three other salespeople before they made their final decision. As a neophyte, I was often the last salesperson interviewed because I was usually the most unknown of the three.

At first I thought this would be a disadvantage, but I quickly found out it was an advantage. By the time I got to the appointment, my prospects would tell me all the mistakes and personality quirks of those salespeople they had interviewed before me. The comment that came up most often was "You are on time. How refreshing."

Then, after the presentation was over, I went to my desk and immediately wrote a thank-you note and made sure it got out in the last mail of the day. If it didn't, I would personally hand-carry the note to the prospect's mailbox so it would be waiting for them the next day.

In the beginning of my career, more often than not, the deciding factor that got me the business was my promptness and my quick reaction time. One of my clients told me later that she had interviewed three very high-powered people before me. By pure coincidence I happened to be cold-calling the area at the time the prospects were on the lookout for a salesperson. Even though these prospects had never heard of me, they figured they would give me a shot at an audition.

Later my newfound clients admitted they had almost decided to use someone else, but out of curiosity wanted to see what I had to say. They were impressed, but the clincher came the following day when none of the other salespeople made follow-up calls or sent notes.

"Your note was in our mailbox first thing in the morning. My husband and I said to each other, 'She's a go-getter. If she follows up like this with us, imagine how fast she will react to prospects.'"

They told me they had serious doubts about the other two salespeople, thinking maybe they were no longer that excited about getting the business. One of the other salesmen did call, but not until three days after I got the order.

KINDLING

A pro sends a handwritten note, and gets his or her letter opened because there is no other handwritten note in the pile of labeled and computerized letters sitting on the customer's desk. Taking the time to handwrite a note is a little act of kindness, and little acts of kindness, and surprise remembrances, go over in a big way with a customer.

I call such acts kindling—kindling the fires of the prospect's loyalty. We become skillful at kindling when we are superb listeners. Listeners always get clues about what makes their clients happy. One of my sales students who is on her way to the big time is always listening for ways to please her people. Recently she began working with an executive and his family who had relocated out west from St. Louis.

Evidently back in their hometown they had a favorite butcher who they claimed sold the best hams anywhere in the world. Every Christmas Eve the wife served one to her family. Except, of course, for this year. My friend had her first appointment with the couple shortly after the holidays, and they were experiencing serious ham withdrawal pains.

This bright saleswoman did some serious investigating after her first appointment with the couple, and found out what butcher shop in St. Louis sold the favorite hams. Then she had one sent to their apartment with a note, "It's not Christmas Eve, but I know you'll enjoy this any day of the year." Needless to say her newfound prospects were more than warmed up for their second appointment with a true kindler.

A previously satisfied customer usually gets this type of treatment but a new prospect is deeply surprised by such generosity. I am not talking about taking every stranger or unqualified prospect out to lunch, or spending money unwisely. On the other hand when we know we are working with sincere people, it's important to give them the message early that we are at their service.

TURN UP THE HEAT WITH ENDORSEMENTS

Many salespeople do not make the most of their past-customer relationships to warm up their present-time prospects. The power of an endorsement made by phone, letter, or in person by one of our biggest supporters—the past customer—will not only speed up the warm-up process, but move us directly into the critical qualifying phase of our work.

In my seminars I often ask the audience how many people have a large supply of testimonial letters from past customers. Time and again the response is very weak, showing not even 1 percent of the audience possessing a respectable collection. The resources are there, but most salespeople do not know how to tap them.

As a new salesperson I was shy, so when a past customer complimented me on a job well done, I did not get the endorsements I needed.

"Well, thank you, Pete. If you get a chance, can you put your comments about my service in writing?"

I was not creating a sense of urgency with people. I didn't realize that when I communicated with most people they were overextended and under a time constraint. One day I responded much more dramatically and got the response I wanted. I still use the same language today to ask for testimonial letters. One spontaneous dialogue said with heartfelt enthusiasm turned into a high-performance sales dialogue.

"I have an urgent request. Can you put your comments in writing about me in the next twenty-four hours?"

Sometimes the client will ask what the rush is.

I answer:

"I go out on a job interview every time I call on a new prospective customer. Who would ever go out on a job interview without a reference letter? I have the power to hire or fire myself every day. Please help me get hired."

When I began asking for an endorsement using that language, and with a sense of urgency in my voice, my collection of letters tripled. Of course I needed to follow up the very next day by calling my client's secretary and volunteering to pick up the letter.

I use endorsement letters when I do in-person presentations

as well as mailings. Besides the letter, I begin educating my past-customer support team, friends, and other strong sponsors of my abilities to make phone calls directly to leads I am working with, prior to a scheduled presentation. When a sponsor of my talents calls a prospect before I do a first presentation, I find the warm-up phase virtually eliminated.

My work as a writer is made so much simpler when I have the luxury of calling on a supporter of mine who happens to be a close friend of an individual I wish to interview for a book. My long-time relationship with Shirley Pepys, CEO of NoJo, Inc., gave me access to female CEOs from the Committee of 200.

With her permission I used her name in my introductory letter, and if I came up against resistance, Shirley put a call in to the woman, or dropped her a note on my behalf.

My credibility skyrockets when Shirley Pepys calls Evelyn Echols or Ellen Gordon of Tootsie Roll, women who have never heard of me, and says, "My very good friend Danielle Kennedy wants to interview you for her book. Please accept her phone call."

It is very critical that my endorser call *before* I make the call, otherwise it could take weeks, maybe months, for me to get past the guard at the gate. Most salespeople just accept the name of a lead from an endorser, never asking for assistance. People today receive from their friends many names of individuals who can provide a service they have a need for, but it is the intermediary call that makes the difference.

The timing of such requests is a sensitive issue. We must earn the right to ask for these types of favors with people. Too many times I have been asked to endorse someone who I did not consider either a close friend or worthy of such an endorsement. Yet that other person had no problem expecting such an endorsement. When we ask people to endorse us, and it is not mutually agreed upon that we are worth the endorsement, we put people in an embarrassing situation.

We know we are in the big time when people not only go out of their way to compliment us, but give us the credit for saving their career. Jim Rhode was in Charlotte, North Carolina, speaking to a dental group when a dentist came up to him and said,

"Jim, you saved my dental career. I was about to quit because my hand hurt so much, and then I bought your special new gloves, and it has made all the difference in the world."

This dentist speaks all over the United States at dental conventions and never forgets to put a plug in for SmartPractice's great glove product. His endorsement comes from the heart and has created hundreds of orders for Rhode's company. All endorsements are powerful, but the endorsements *of* the powerful can dramatically improve our positioning in our field.

The endorsement of those who appear to be the not-so-powerful is equally as important. Many assistants to the president and secretaries have helped me in the warm-up phase with a customer. During college, I would work as a secretary, and I was always amazed by the way the caller would talk to me. He or she seemed unaware of the amount of influence I had on whether the call would go through or get returned.

I've used my "Guard at the Gate" dialogue for years to warm up all parties concerned. Here's how it works.

When I call the company, I ask the receptionist for the name of the secretary of the party I am calling. If she tells me her name is Polly, I ask to be connected to Polly.

"Hi, Polly," I say. "My name is Danielle Kennedy. I know you must be really busy, so I will get to the point. I understand Mr. Johnson is interviewing different reps because you are about to update your system. When do you think the best time would be to call back and ask him a few questions, so I can customize a proposal?"

I find the secretary often says, "Oh, he's here right now. I'll connect you." Or the worst might be: "If you call him back about four o'clock he will have a better opportunity to discuss this with you."

Secretaries appreciate people who call and do not act as if they are the most important callers of the day. They like men and women who tell the truth and do not expect busy secretaries and their bosses to drop everything they are doing because Mr. or Mrs. Important is on the line and wants some fast action. Not only am I appreciated because of my behavior, but I have created a built-in helper (the secretary) to assist me during the crucial warm-up phase of the sales process.

What could be a better send-off than a highly respected secretary saying to her boss, "You have to talk to this woman. She is so kind and courteous and really sounds like she knows what she is talking about."

OPENING RELATIONSHIPS WITH CLOSING QUESTIONS

Creating excitement, differentiation, speed, endorsements, and kindling all create the makings of a terrific warm-up, but nothing will prepare us more for a spectacular presentation than knowing how to ask the right questions. I frequently get ideas from watching professional interviewers.

One of my favorites is Maria Shriver. I once watched her ask in an extremely tactful manner a very personal question of a successful rock star who was raised in the ghetto by a single mother. This is not a direct quote, but I remember the word "temptation" was used in the questioning. She worded it something like this:

"In your neighborhood the temptation to take drugs was all around you. How did you handle and overcome these temptations?"

The star agreed there were temptations, and he was tempted many times, but his mother worked very hard for all eight of his brothers and sisters, and he knew it would break her heart if he tried drugs.

Shriver's voice was warm and compassionate and her choice of words was very appropriate. The key word was "temptation."

She did not make the man feel as if his desires were any different from those of anyone else who might have been living in the same situation. He was human, therefore he was tempted.

An unspoken question floating through the air at every encounter with a prospect is "Are we compatible?" If the prospect and I are compatible, the trust will build. I stick with open-ended questions that require me to do most of the listening.

What are your needs?

How can I be of help?

What is your time frame on this?

This is the type of question I use to draw lifetime customers in. Years of experience has given me the confidence to say,

"At this juncture we are just getting to know each other. Neither of us knows yet if this is going to be a fit. That's why I want you to tell me exactly what you need so I can determine what is in your best interests."

Host of current radio program "Selling Across America," author and former Hewlett Packard (HP) sales star Tony Parinello told me it was only after his presentation was given a deadline that he learned how to begin an interview with closing questions.

"I did some research about a man by the name of Mr. Dean who was president of the largest one-hour photo development company in the United States and the first person to franchise one-hour photo development. His company had a big need for expensive computer equipment and HP appeared to be the perfect fit.

"I cold-called him and got him on the line. He told me I could come up and talk to him but for only ten minutes. I remember walking into his office. It looked like a museum. I remember thinking to myself that there were plenty of ice-breaking questions I could ask about his office alone, but with a ten-minute deadline I needed to cut to the chase."

Parinello began with a question that had worked for him in the past.

"What are your goals and objectives regarding the efficiency of your operation between now and the end of the year?"

Then Tony asked Dean to fill in the blanks. Tony specified a time frame in his question so Dean would not think he had to waste time educating Tony about his entire operation. Busy company presidents do not have time for unprepared sales-people.

"It took Mr. Dean the entire ten minutes to answer the question. Just as he was about to wrap up his answer, he stood up and moved toward the door, telling me our ten minutes was up.

"It was a fairly big office, so I attempted to dash toward the door, but my briefcase was on my lap. I tried to close the case and my tie and jacket got caught inside of it. I was fumbling my way over and somehow managed to blurt out a thank-you while telling him how honored I was to have spent the ten minutes with him. Then I asked him about the weird painting on his wall. I said, 'I know my time is up, Mr. Dean, but I am curious. How does the painting on your wall apply to your business?' "

It was of Jack Murphy Stadium in San Diego. There was a crowd of people holding up banners in the bleachers, and in the forefront of the stadium was a 1961 Chevrolet Impala hardtop with the front wheels off the ground. The car appeared to be moving up and down. There was someone on the ground with a yardstick, and another person looking to see how far up and down the car was moving.

Dean told him that in San Diego they have a contest. People put hydraulic shocks in the front of the car so the car can bounce up and down. The one that bounces the highest wins.

"I get this Colombo-type confused look on my face and ask him again how this applied to his business. Then he told me that he has his own yardstick, and when people come into his office with a new idea, he measures how high they jump, and the person who jumps the highest wins."

That's all Tony needed to hear. He automatically responded by asking Dean "to share with me the elements of your personal yardstick."

Dean invited Tony to sit back down on the couch and for the next forty-five minutes, Dean shared exactly what Tony had to do to meet the criteria for doing business with his company.

"From that one experience I took that question and have found it to be the most successful investigative question I could ask busy executives: 'How high do I have to jump up on your yardstick to earn the right to do business with you?' Dean was specific. I knew when I walked out of there why I wouldn't get the business. But the beauty of that question is it tells us exactly *how* to get the business, and when we don't get it, we have no one to blame but ourselves, because the prospect has made it clear from the beginning what he or she is seeking."

Chapter Four Review

- Don't stop business developing, even on days when you have plenty of presentations. Knowing you have other prospects in the loop makes you feel more confident during presentations.
- Develop the walk-in-like-you-own-the-place mind-set.
- Concentrate on how familiar, not foreign, each prospect you call on is to you.
- The warm-up starts with the proper mind-set.
- Remember you have a mission to accomplish.
- Create excitement. It generates certainty.

- Look for opportunities everywhere to generate excitement.
- Give away free gifts and events.
- Create warm feelings of friendship and family.
- Performance presentations are not spontaneous events.
- Practice makes perfect.
- Take risks during the preparatory stage.
- Differentiation demands preparation.
- Prepare by researching who your customers are and what they need and want.
- Focus your presentation on results.
- Emphasize ethical standards in your presentation.
- Prepare, but get the credit for going the extra mile.
- Focus groups empower your preparatory work.
- When in doubt, ask the customer.
- Knowledge of both big and small details polishes presentations.
- Periodically call on past customers without asking for anything.
- Craft a product story.
- Submit proposals that are very specific.
- Emphasize the extent of your experience level.
- Behave like a servant at your presentation.
- Sell and remember.
- React fast and impress your customer, who is used to slow response.
- Be on time.
- Send handwritten notes.
- Listen more.
- Collect endorsements.
- Ask your supporters to call ahead for you.

- Ask the right questions at the right time.
- Find out if you and the customer are compatible.
- Know what it takes to measure up to your customer's expectations.

THE BIG DIFFERENCE: THE POWER OF PERFORMANCE PRESENTATION

"My fears led me to feel an obligation to interest the audience. This feeling of obligation interferred with my throwing myself into what I was doing."

—CONSTANTIN STANISLAVSKI, AN ACTOR PREPARES

WE WALK into a presentation with either one of the following mind-sets: the I-am-here-to-sell-you mind-set or the I-am-here-to-serve-you mind-set.

The sell mind-set has been around for about a hundred years: "We are making as many products as we can for you, and we intend to sell them to you as fast as possible, for the highest possible price, and then we are out the door. So whatever you do, don't complain or ask any questions. We know you are sort of dumb, so it is easy to wow you, because you can be talked into anything."

A lot of business is still being done with the sell-'em-fast-and-sell-'em-hard mind-set, but the service mind-set is on the rise because the buyer is not a dummy. He no longer will stand by and be wowed by some insulting product peddler.

Today the customer is talking back to the salesperson boldly:

"Look, you are going to have to get to know me before I fork over a wad of money your way. Start listening to me, understanding my little quirks and habits, and never forget that you are not the only fish in the ocean. There is always someone smarter out there than you, selling better technology, and more than willing to impress the pants off me."

The service ethic all boils down to trust. Trust creates the relationship. Trust creates sales, and more trust reinforced creates more business.

The consumer is not impressed with just one single dazzling presentation, but a history of trust-building steps. This growing trust eventually bonds him or her to a partner who shares a joint interest in making a win-win collaboration work.

NoJo's Shirley Pepys says, "You can close the sale without selling the client a thing. This was very true when we landed the Toys R Us account. I was over in Europe, and at the time I was president of the Juvenile Products Association. We were in Germany and the buyer for Toys R Us was there too. I sincerely liked the buyer and staff, and I knew the feelings were mutual.

"I was having great fun with these people in a nonworking atmosphere. So by the time I left Germany I was thrilled, really on a high, because I knew we had made a lasting connection. There was no phoniness between us. I truly enjoyed being with them, and I still do."

ACT TO SELL

When passion and preparation energize technique, history-making performance presentation is the result. For thirty-two years of his life and some 4,637 performances in *The King and I*, the late actor Yul Brynner showed the world what history-making performance—sales performance—was all about. During the final four months of his performances at the Pantages Theatre in Los Angeles, he played the King at night, but lived by day as a sick and dying man receiving chemotherapy for his terminal cancer.

Nobody thought of Yul Brynner as a salesman, but he was. He consistently transmitted to the audience the thoughts, feelings, and words of another, by making his audience believe he was a strong and stubborn king, perhaps even forgetting himself during those final performances.

Although I possessed somewhat of an unconscious competence regarding my sales abilities in the early days of my career, reflecting back I realize it was my acting ability that moved me along in my sales progress. Each time I talked to a new prospect, my passion drove me to lose a little of myself and become a little bit more of my prospect.

Such habits of transference drove my family crazy because during the time periods I worked with certain customers, I took on their mannerisms and behaviors. I found myself hating what my customers hated, loving what they loved, and understanding their reasons for doing so. I prided myself on my ability to extract the truth from my prospects, and to internally receive and accept the feelings, thoughts, and logic they transmitted to me through their outward personalities and behavior.

Years ago, when I began teaching other salespeople what I did that made me successful, I had a very difficult time explaining how I was able to present and close millions of dollars in sales. This is common among peak performers, as well as actors. In the book *Acting—The First Six Lessons*, it is written, "Often he [the actor] does not know what it is he does or how he does it, that makes him an actor. He can only express it in action."

This is why it is critical in sales training to go beyond mere role-playing to teach effective sales skills. At my own company

I always insisted on using opportunities of observing either myself or other top producers in action in order to learn. I never found role-playing helpful because the experiences were fake. Whereas with role-modeling the new salesperson accompanies the peak performer out on the firing line, and watches how that salesperson digs deep into the psyche of the prospect and personally takes on the client's needs.

A good actor *becomes* the character. A good salesperson *becomes* the prospect. This act of becoming is rooted in the salesperson's personal passion to produce quality work, which drives the external technique—technique meaning "manner of accomplishing something." In selling, the noticeable difference between mediocre presentations and performance presentations is the craft of *becoming*—becoming the product or service.

There is no way to teach this transforming ability, but our personal awareness of *becoming* the client is critical. When we begin to see things through the customer's eyes, we take our mind off our own likes, dislikes, and interests. Because we have no agendas or selfish motives, our presentation will have a sense of purity about it. We feel it when we have it. It's recognizable when it's real.

Josie Natori says, "What I sell is part of who I am. You are not truly selling when you are faking it. It must be a part of yourself. It has to come from your insides, so that when it comes out it is very natural."

Part of who we are is made up of our belief system. There are plenty of fair-to-good salespeople that can get by selling something they do not necessarily believe in or feel passionate about, but the end result is they are doing just that—getting by.

Lane Nemeth says, "You do not have to be a qualified salesperson with a twelve-year history of selling to do well as an educational consultant at Discovery Toys. I was just a mother with a toddler when I started selling. I knew my product and deeply cared about it. My passion translated into enthusiasm, and without enthusiasm, all the technique in the world can't help a flat presentation."

Although the great salesperson has suitcases full of techniques accumulated through years of sales experience, he or she, like the talented actor, only brings to a particular presentation the tools that are needed. The mediocre find it necessary to recite clever dialogues that only seem to bore the prospect. The *act-to-sell* salesperson becomes so sensitive to the prospect's desires that he or she only speaks of those issues in the presentation that will make sense to the prospect.

MAKING CONTACT AND AROUSING DESIRE

We make contact with the prospect when we not only gain their attention, but deeply arouse their desire for our product. All it took during a presentation from a Discovery Toy Emerald Manager (a top-producing manager) to arouse a recruit's deepest desires for a new life as a Discovery Toy consultant was the following very personalized language:

"This career will give you more time with your little girl, and the opportunity to never have to drive three hours to work again."

The prospective recruit was a police officer who was deeply motivated to change her lifestyle.

"I was leaving my little one off at five o'clock every morning at a day-care center and not returning until 7:00 in the evening. The drive alone was two hours each way. I was totally fed up and truly ready for somebody to convince me that there was a better way."

The reason many mediocre salespeople never improve their sales statistics is that they have never discovered the true motivation of their prospects. This hole in the presentation leads to focusing on the wrong features of the product, features that are of no interest to the prospect. All this feature selling is sales exhibitionism. For example, the police officer cares about the child development research conducted at Discovery Toys, but not that much. Maybe she already trusts the quality of the product. It is not the issue that needs to be spotlighted, and if the star sales director doesn't know that yet, then she is not going to make a conversion.

"You have to convert the people," says Lane Nemeth. "It was the masterful interviewing and listening skills of our Diamond Directors that took them to the big time."

These are women who earn millions selling educational toys out of their homes. These are star-studded professionals who know how to convert thousands of people into their downlines.

Conversion means "a change of heart." The prospect walks in with one point of view, and if he or she doesn't walk out with the same one the salesperson has, or at least a tad closer than when the prospect walked in, there will be no sale.

Blue Diamond performer Nathan Rich of NuSkin says they have built a company around the "baby boomers who are freaked out about getting old. The Youth Generation. The Woodstock Crowd."

The closer the product or the service comes to the very heart of a deep human concern, the higher the rate of conversion. NuSkin, from its inception, went right to the point of contact with the consumer. They struck a nerve, made a deep impression, and then implemented what President Blake Roney calls "personal retailing" to arouse consumer desire.

NuSkin people claim some of the big cosmetic companies are beginning to realize they are losing people because they do not have the opportunity to explain the uniqueness of their product. With personal retailing, the NuSkin rep has the opportunity to go right into the home of the consumer and create some very special effects.

Founder Sandie Tillotson says, "I believed in NuSkin from the beginning. Myself, Blake's sister Nedra, and Blake were the first distributors. We used to do demonstrations with sixty people at a time stretched out on somebody's living room floor while we painted half their face with our nonsurgical face-lift. Fifteen minutes later they would all be looking at themselves in the mirror admiring the very noticeable difference. Our biggest problem was trying to fill the orders fast enough."

Tillotson says NuSkin needs to be explained and demonstrated.

"It isn't a typical skin care line with one or two good ingredients max, and the rest of the product containing only fillers, mineral oils, and harsh alcohols. It contains sophisticated sunscreens, preservative systems, and natural fragrances, all of which require explaining."

Each ingredient has a hot-button benefit for the consumer. But NuSkin is a network marketing company too, so how can they make contact and present to a recruit?

"Seamless competition," says International V.P. Renn Patch, "is what differentiates us, and immediately arouses the interest of the prospective distributor during the recruiting interview.

"Through international sponsoring, a distributor in any of the open markets around the world can sponsor an individual, allowing that distributor to build on his or her existing efforts. For example, if a U.S. distributor has relatives in Japan, he or she can tack those relatives onto his or her downline without having to start over."

One of the biggest problems in marketing products or services today is wrong targeting—going after the wrong prospect with what the marketing department thinks is the right program.

"This is what happens when there are too many middlemen," says Shirley Pepys. "Too many people stand in the way between the manufacturer and the consumer. There must be a clear pipeline between the two, otherwise conversion becomes incomprehensible."

TEAMWORK AND THE PLANNING
SESSION PRESENTATION

Depending on the industry, some of the most passionate and prepared of performers rarely fly solo. They know that creating partnership means making a lasting contact. When we find ourselves in the boardroom presenting our service or goods to people whom we have taken the time to study, listen to, and get to know, with the expressed goal of "joint interest" being very openly communicated to all participants, the chances of us and our company outshining the self-absorbed competition dramatically improves.

David Steitz, president of Characters, Inc., a multimillion dollar computer typesetting business in Houston, Texas, uses the team sales and planning approach to win over his clients during tough presentations.

"There was a case where we had a large catalog to do for a customer, and we had never dealt with them before. So what we developed was a team of six people in our company from various disciplines. The team included myself, the sales representative, the customer service representative, the technical computer specialist, the trainer, and the software specialist meeting with our client," says David.

The sales rep and David were only there to facilitate the discussion and introduce the other team members. All during the presentation, which was conducted much more like a planning session than a sales presentation, each one of the team members gave a presentation of his or her role in the project as if already doing the job.

Steitz says, "I wish I could tell you that this was all done intentionally but it just happened that way. My other team members were not salespeople—they were just folks that do the work, and do it well. This fact came across brilliantly and we ended up going from what was supposed to be a sales presentation, to a planning meeting, to scheduling with the prospects when we could actually start the project. It was magical."

The beauty of team performance is there are enough experts in the room explaining their role in the project to handle bona fide objections by the client. However, sometimes a salesperson does not get the opportunity Steitz and his team got to represent themselves to the decision makers. So a partnership must be formed with the contact person who will be doing the presentation on your behalf in your absence.

Recently, I found myself in a similar position with a meeting planner of a large cosmetic company who had attended one of my new business theater speeches and was very enthused to have me present it at her company's next convention. My company provided her with a video demonstration of the address.

She was worried that what she received did not do the program justice, and she wanted to go into that committee meeting armed with the best tools she could in order to sell me. I would not have the advantage of being able to sell my program to the committee, so it was up to my new partner to get my message across effectively.

If I could accommodate her needs prior to her presentation to the committee of decision makers, then her chances of delivering a performance presentation to her boss and the other decision-makers would go up dramatically, and so would my chances of being selected to do the program. I closed the order by using the following two-step spproach to partnering:

1. Don't Take Offense; Take Action.

I asked the contact person to be honest with me after she saw the video of my new program. She loved 75 percent of it, but felt it needed more excerpts of both my actual speech and the transition into musical moments, as well as multimedia samplings. She explained to me that corporate America can be very conservative and this tape smelled a little too much of hype and show business and not enough of how-to and real world business.

She had the advantage of having heard me lecture and seen the program live, so she knew that this impression from the tape would be erroneous, but her boss might make a false judgment on what he saw.

It's a tough pill to swallow when we come out of the editing room with what our own pride tells us is a first-class creation, and the market is telling us it needs a bit of fixing. But I asked for a candid response, and this woman and I had formed an unspoken partnership. I knew trying to take her suggestions was the least I could do for a buddy who was trying to get a program through that was over budget and riskier than the norm.

I took the necessary action, working on a better video presentation and a clearly defined one-page marketing piece that took her suggestions into consideration. I had to move quickly because the big meeting day was fast approaching. My willingness and speed of reaction time bonded our partnership even deeper.

2. *Offer Options Galore.*

In today's marketplace you must be product rich. I knew that if my "Broadway Keynote" wouldn't fly for her during that committee meeting, I needed to provide her with other programs I could deliver. So I gave her the straight keynote option, the half-day sales training option, the full-day sales training option, and the three-day management opportunity.

I discussed how we could use multimedia at their convention. I could personalize my program with video vignettes of their sales team and executives on a rear-screen projector, tying them in with my presentation and giving the entire program a very personalized touch.

She also mentioned that the president needed a bilingual

speaker for one of the slots at the convention. The speaker's fee would figure into the overall budget and decision regarding which of my two keynotes they could afford. As a board member of the National Speakers Association, I was able to recommend some solid speakers, allowing her to walk into the meeting with specifics about fees for a bilingual speaker. If she and I had not formed a "joint interest" relationship, I sincerely doubt she would have told me about all the other possible objections that would be coming up at that meeting.

When we give our clients something new, something that will help them make a competitive breakthrough in their business, we increase our chances for closing the deal. When we offer tham something that they do not presently have, but need in order to be strategically successful, everybody ends up winning.

David Steitz's team had studied the way their prospective clients had done business in the past. So during their presentation/planning session they not only demonstrated that they had an understanding of the existing process, but offered a new unique value.

David says, "This sent an important message over to the client: 'We are willing to go beyond the original specifications.' "

TRUE STORIES BUILD TRUST

If we are not telling stories, we are not giving power presentations. The prospect's viewpoint about our service must change during the interaction. The passionate feelings that are aroused in both the salesperson and the buyer when stories are told often lead to conversion and decisions to buy.

Henry Rogers in his book *Rogers' Rules for Success* tells about the time Shirley MacLaine's television special was pitched by his account executives at Rogers and Cowan and rejected.

Rogers and MacLaine put their heads together and decided to call the president of *Time* himself and offer to bring Shirley over to dinner with the president's wife, a big Shirley MacLaine fan. After dinner Shirley told the whole story of her show, how she got the idea, and then performed it in the living room. The couple was spellbound. The show was aired, and *Time* magazine was the sponsor.

Ruth Mayer, famed Laguna beach artist, walked into her gallery two weeks before Christmas one year as my husband and I were contemplating buying a limited edition serigraph she had completed of Avalon Harbor on Catalina Island. Several lookers were standing around the picture when she walked up to us and introduced herself.

She asked if anybody in her studio had told us the "story behind this painting." That question alone aroused our desire and created an instant connection with both the art and the artist.

Then she told us how she flew over to Catalina on Christmas morning the year before (she is a pilot) and photographed the harbor on what happened to be one of the clearest mornings of the year. For the next eighteen months with a pallet knife and 123 different colors she spent countless hours in her studio completing the painting we were all admiring.

I liked the painting before I heard that story, but after meeting her and hearing the story, I *had* to have that painting. Three others who stood by listening felt the same way. I know Ruth does not like to think of herself as a salesperson, but that day the artist and the storyteller merged into one of the best saleswomen I've heard.

NoJo's Shirley Pepys says, "Our story creates sales, loyal customers, and good feelings about us in the industry."

Shirley says when the reps are on the road they do not have the advantage of taking a lot of product with them.

"There is no wonderful crib or vignette setting to work with.

We advise our new people not to take any product into the customer the first few times. The rep should be asking questions, getting to know the people, and telling the NoJo story. Then comes the product on the third or fourth visit."

That is how Shirley and her former partner Sylvia Noble sold NoJo in the early years. Shirley remembers calling on one of the toughest buyers in the department store business and landing the account because they played themselves down and told their true story.

"We heard about how tough this woman was, and we already knew that she was almost impossible to get a hold of in order to schedule an appointment. I will never forget the first time we met her. She was as grumpy as can be, and there was a sign behind her that read 'ASSUME NOTHING.' She looked like a sergeant in the military. Written all over her was 'Don't think you can come in here and sell me something.'

"We didn't try to dazzle her. We just spent time with her telling our story—why we created these infant seat covers, our little success and failure experiences, etc. We asked her things like 'Would you be happy sleeping on plastic? Vinyl? Well, neither would your baby.' It was so satisfying watching her melt. I wanted to turn that sign behind her around when I left her office that day.

"Neither of us knew that much about selling at the time, and we were letting our gut guide us. If we had tried to be anything more than human, we never would have landed that account or discovered a lasting friendship with that buyer."

Telling the story has cost NuSkin millions of well-spent dollars. NuSkin's headquarters in Provo, Utah, has a dramatic first floor design which centers around the NuSkin story and mission. It was designed this way on purpose in order to impress potential distributors.

An impressive display tells the story of Ponce de León's quest for the fountain of youth. Another features pages out of the early scrapbook of NuSkin history. When NuSkin began,

Blake Roney says, "People had to bring their own containers to our garage. In they walked with baby food jars and Tic-Tac containers, and we would spoon the lotion out of gallon vats. It was strictly word of mouth presenting and selling."

Potential distributors receive tours, hear the story, and are not only told but can see for themselves that NuSkin is financially solvent—an important concern to the MLM recruit. The 260,000-square-foot distribution center, sophisticated computer and voice mail systems, as well as first-class printed materials, featuring their Blue Diamond Distributors and their individual human interest profiles, are all part of the evidence. This is how NuSkin creates a strong bond between the company and its vast distributor force.

Joey Tamer says, "I tell a lot of stories when I am both negotiating and closing. Success stories, never failure stories such as 'This is what happened to a company that didn't hire me for my services. Today they are all living on park benches.'

"One company in particular allows me to discuss their successful results anytime I want. I met with them in the planning stages, and we developed their business plan. When they were ready to go forward, however, they found they had spent most of their money on product development, and they had no money for distribution. They needed advance money for distribution. I recommended they sell equity in the company before it was highly valued—at its weakest moment of evaluation.

"Then I got them the largest deal in distribution ever done. Ten months later they sold 20 percent of their company for $5 million, with an evaluation of $25 million. They were happy they called me up. We have been tracking the business plan, and eighteen months later we are within 2 percent of accuracy. Tell me that story hasn't gotten me a ton of other business."

Brenda Burke, Vice President of Sales and Marketing for Pecos River Learning Centers, uses stories about past customers who have helped her "grow her future business."

"John Mayberry, CEO of Defasco, Inc., a steel company in Canada, is a true champion of our cause. Defasco's team have all experienced the curriculum [at Pecos River Learning Center], and the changes are too numerous to mention. He is the man that makes personal calls for me to Fortune 500 Company presidents praising the work we do at Pecos.

"Kodak produced a video and wrote a book called *Team Zebra* about our experiences together. I shared the Kodak story with John at Defasco before they came on board. Stories being told by the right people at the right time have created my rich sales history at Pecos."

REAL EVIDENCE BUILDS CREDIBILITY

"Storytelling and physical evidence produce the credibility," advises David Steitz, especially when we hear the common objection: We are happy with our current product or who we are using.

"The truth is most consumers are using people they are happy with when a new, unproven salesperson arrives on the scene. One way that we dealt with this problem during a presentation was by producing physical evidence of quality work and letting that work speak for itself.

"We were making a pitch to an ad agency to do an annual report for them. They had never used us before, let alone let us take on such a big project. We had been in business for several years and we had done many annual reports, yet this client did not perceive us in that category of supplier. They saw us as the little jobs company.

"So my salesperson and I gathered together samples of every annual report we had done. It was about an eight-inch-tall stack. We carried the stack into the customer's office and sat down across from his desk. Then we made our presentation in terms of what our proposed turnaround time would be and what value we would bring to the report. Then we specified how we would handle the process, how much it would cost, and the end result that could be expected.

"We never alluded to this stack of annual reports. We just let it sit there. The entire time the customer just kept looking at the stack as if it was going to jump down and bite him."

We'll read about how David and the team concluded that presentation later in this chapter.

PREDICTABLE PATTERNS OF BUYING BEHAVIOR

Being a prepared pro with the mind-set of a giver is only half the challenge of performance presentation. The other half is educating ourselves on the sometimes subconscious process that leads bona fide prospects to the buying decision. We must observe the thoughts and actions of those we serve. Are our prospects in the buying mood during our presentation? The buyer's attitude, budget, price point, and other circumstances, determine how long it takes the prospect to move through the following behaviors:

1. Taking Time to Explore

Sharon D'Orsie knows that "It takes a lot of time to sow seeds in my business. Sometimes over a year." So she takes an initial position with the prospect that she is coming on the scene as a resource to tap.

"During the getting acquainted stage with the prospect, a good salesperson is like an open dictionary. The prospect is using the salesperson to look up answers and define parts of the product or service that need more explanation."

Several activities are happening at the same time in the exploratory stage. The prospect is checking us out, our company, the team, and our product, but we should be doing some checking of our own. Is this prospect someone I want to work with? Will we make a good fit long term?

I learned the hard way how to screen and explore a prospect. After a disappointing relationship with a prospect that lied to me about their true buying intentions, I realized I had spent several months with unmotivated prospects. Immediately following that heartbreaking incident, I learned my lesson and put some common sense into my early communications with new prospects.

From that heartbreaking time forward I spontaneously delivered the following message to those I worked with:

"Promise me you will be honest with me today. Tell me exactly what your budget, time frame, and needs are, and I will do everything in my power to find the perfect fit for you. Neither of us can be sure if things will work out, but that is not my concern right now. Most important is that you feel comfortable enough with me to tell me exactly where you stand, so I can properly advise and serve you."

That bit of a dissertation is the smartest thing I could ever say to a new prospect. It puts them at ease and automatically gives them permission to tell me the truth about their intentions to buy.

When I sell my services as a consultant, the initial phase is more of a time for me to send out signals that I am interested in the job, and a time for me to ask a few directed questions. It may seem obvious that the client knows I am interested, but often this aspect is overlooked.

"I think I could contribute to your overall training environment and produce some systems that could secure your position in U.S. sales" was the way I opened a dialogue with a large foreign-based hair-care company president.

Then he confided in me about some of the company's sales weaknesses and what they might "be interested in pursuing" should we decide to work with each other. I learned early on that their budget would only permit audio training at first, but if sales proved successful, we could move on to producing a more extensive and expensive video library. I tailored my questions in that first discussion by asking "why" most of the time. That way I got specific answers from the customer.

Our biggest job is to get to the truth as quickly as possible with a prospect. Average salespeople just try to close the sale. Pros probe for the truth about what is motivating a prospect. We realize that if we know the absolute truth, eventually we will close the sale.

One of the best things that happens to us is the help we receive from mentors during the sales process, particularly helpful during the critical early exploratory stages.

John Marconi advises to use mentors whenever possible to build our credibility.

"Early on in your presentation when you mention a name that the prospect respects, you receive almost instant credibility. Having mentors has worked for me at every stage of my career. When I started my own business, it was necessary for me to go sell myself to the banks to get loans anywhere from a quarter of a million dollars on up.

"I was barely thirty years old. I did not get thrown out the door because my mentor gave me the clout, the credibility."

Mentors teach us the political system of a company too. In the introductory stages of the presentation it helps if we know how that company's system works. Mentors are full of experience and can provide us not only with the connections, but valuable "how to's" of getting to a prospect.

SmartPractice president Jim Rhode says his brother-in-law the dentist was his first mentor and teacher.

"He taught me the dental business. Without his guidance I would not have known who my customer really was."

2. Slight Withdrawal

The head of the hair-care company I mentioned earlier made a comment during our presentation that earlier in my career I would have interpreted as discouraging, but now I know he was acting true to form.

He said, "Let's get back in touch with each other in about the middle of August and see if there is any interest on our part or yours."

During the next several weeks I was able to give the project serious thought, do my research on cost projections, and be realistic about what I could accomplish for the company given a certain time frame. I have watched some salespeople behave very impulsively, make promises that were unrealistic and could not be kept, and try to get the prospect to make a quicker decision. Ultimately in that case future opportunities are doomed early on, due to the salesperson's lack of patience.

Timing is everything. If we experience a put-off from the client, or an expression of withdrawal in any form, we must learn to be able to continue through that stage of the relationship. Remember people change their minds daily, and the slight withdrawal is only temporary. Whether we are selling people on our product or trying to recruit/sponsor them into our downline sales organization, taking a few steps back is often part of the process.

Remember some prospects react enthusiastically from the outset about a new idea or product, but most refrain from early excitement. People have become skeptical because of bad past sales experiences. They carry those experiences, basic personality traits, background, parental influence, and financial viewpoints with them into the present moment.

They may not be aware enough or ready yet to accept a particular part of our sales talk that could influence them more effectively in the future. Nathan Rich, who ended up becoming one of the Blue Diamond Distributors (the highest ranking sales level) at NuSkin International, took more than a few steps back in the beginning of his career, resisting a future that has turned out very rosy.

"I sold NuSkin for about six months and then I quit because I did not think the company was going to make it. I just began thinking negative and telling myself that most network marketing companies didn't make it anyway. I convinced myself I was wasting my time."

Then four years later he was selling commerical real estate in Los Angeles when his brother-in-law recruited him for the second time.

"I remember he told me that NuSkin was taking off and he asked me where else I thought I could have the potential of making $30,000 a month? I told him I thought I could do that selling commercial real estate. Then he said, 'Yeah, but you can't do it every month.'

"Maybe it was the timing. Maybe it was the stage of development NuSkin was at and where my head was, but it just started making more sense to me than it did in the past."

Nathan's brother-in-law was persistent and it paid off. Too many salespeople become discouraged at the prospect's first sign of resistance.

How many times have we disqualified ourselves unnecessarily?

3. More Questions and Answers

Nathan's brother-in-law got to Nathan where he lived, down deep at his point of contact—where a change of heart, mind, or viewpoint takes place for a prospective buyer.

"I just started changing my mind. For me to make $30,000 selling real estate, I would have to do everything myself. But with a strong downline, others could be bringing in that kind of money for me monthly. So I started asking a whole bunch of questions."

Nathan's brother-in-law arranged a tour of NuSkin and had a list of prospering distributors and testimonial letters at his fingertips. He was also familiar with their fault tolerant computer system, which is an important issue to people who consider joining a network marketing company.

"When a distributor calls in, the order is entered, and the

computer calculates the best way to mail the products. The order is shipped out within twenty-four hours. This kind of backup meant a lot to me because I had once been a part of a multilevel marketing company that couldn't pay its bills, let alone ship my customer's product or write my paychecks on time."

His brother-in-law specifically included the fact that no one had ever been not paid or late being paid since the inception of the company. The owners were fanatics about paying their people on time.

If he had started talking to Nathan about the natural ingredients of the product, or the credibility of the dermatologist who endorses the product, his message would not have made a difference to Nathan. But instead he made his points because he knew *how* to use his knowledge in an appropriate manner. As simple as this example seems, most salespeople do not know how to select the correct information from their knowledge bank, or how to ask razor-edge questions, and fill in the specific blanks that pertain to a customer.

In this phase, it is not necessary to hammer the point home with the prospect, but simply to deliver the right facts confidently. It is important not to bring up additional questions or information that don't pertain to the prospect's needs.

A keen memory helps too, but Jim Rhode says note taking is a must for the sharpest of minds. Otherwise major mistakes can be made later in the sales process.

"If I am talking to a dentist and find out during this question-and-answer phase that he is very anti–nitrous oxide, I am going to code his record when I go back to the office, so I never bring up this touchy subject again. 'How many times do I have to tell you I don't use nitrous oxide with my patients' is not the kind of feedback a sales legend needs to hear from his customer."

4. Pondering and Brainstorming

Once again the perfect opportunity to tell a story presents itself. Nathan learned the art of storytelling from his brother-in-law, who recruited him, and now he applies the art in his own presentations.

"There's a dentist here in Provo that tried to shovel the snow off his roof last winter after a bad storm and accidentally fell off the roof and broke both arms. What do you do when you are a dentist and you break both arms? This man could have lost his house, lost everything. But he had a side income from NuSkin that earned him about $3,000 a month, which put the food on his table and made his house payment."

A powerful presentation story gets the prospect thinking, and sometimes talking out loud to himself, or talking to the members of the family, or to the decision-making team who are present.

It's important to tell the story and then shut up. Many salespeople try to jump in the middle of the prospect's self-talk or brainstorming session with other members of the decision-making committee. Let people vent, express themselves, and even make negative comments. Later, when we see the entire picture, those comments may be understood as meaningless.

Our prospects may be saying things like "But if we put this new computer system in, something will have to be taken out of the budget. Remember we promised ourselves we wouldn't mess with our budget this year."

In the next breath the prospect is already talking about ways to cut back to make room for our product or service. If we tried to jump in the middle of the committee's conversation or the individual's self-talk, we would truly weaken our sales case. Just let them ponder, brainstorm, and discuss the ins and the outs.

5. More Doubts and Questions

Right before he made his commitment to NuSkin, Nathan Rich's own fear started rearing its ugly head.

"I brought up all the losing MLM companies to my brother-in-law and came up with even more reasons to shoot his recruiting effort down. But he remained steadfast and handled every question I brought to his attention. Listening to him made me want to become as knowledgeable and self-assured as he was.

"For example, I hated the way MLM companies expanded to new territories and other countries but did not allow the distributor to sponsor their overseas relative. He told me about the 'seamless plan' that allows a Japanese family in California to expand their downline in Japan when their relative in Japan opens a NuSkin business. That made so much sense to me not to have to start over. There are a lot of salespeople who do not know enough about their company's basic policies and plans, and in the interim they are losing hundreds of recruits."

This step is often eliminated in smaller ticket purchases, but when people are spending millions of dollars for computers or considering making a major career change, stakes go up and the decision time is longer and more intensely thought out. The pros know patience is a virtue.

Sharon D'Orsie knows "it sometimes takes a year or two for a seed to sprout. But we hang in there by calling and sending notes, always subtly getting the message across that we are not going anywhere. This reminds prospects that our credibility is high, and we are just a phone call away if a question comes up. Exemplifying that quiet confidence alone impresses our prospects to no end."

6. Resolution

Resolution is another way of saying closing the sale. Sometimes very little has to be said at the time of resolution and no formal closing of the sale is necessary.

David Steitz says, "I really think you have to read the person. Some people are very action oriented, and they would appreciate the close on the spot. Others are very analytical and really like to gather many facts and supporting information."

Some prospects enjoy analyzing all the options even when they have resolved in their minds what they are probably going to buy. So one of these people is not going to like it if a salesperson comes on the scene and tries to put the abrupt close on before the prospect has examined other options. No matter how much prospects like this may love the offering, they are going to resist resolution at this point in their thinking.

When David Steitz and his associate did a presentation for the advertising agency mentioned earlier, they walked in with their eight-inch stack of annual reports and went for it.

"The fact that we didn't say anything, but just let the reports sit there was dramatic. At the end of the presentation we simply said, 'Do you see any reason why you would not use us on your report?' He looked at the pile and he looked at us and said, 'No, and we are going to use you.'"

The bottom line is we need to know who our customers are. If they are the type that need incubation time, we have to pace ourselves to that customer's need. Other customers have that "do it now" style, and sometimes customer abruptness can throw even the best off base a bit. Steitz remembers calling on the head of a company who happened to be a very intimidating man.

"One of those that, if he could, would scare you out of his office. Yet we went ahead and gave him our presentation to do his company brochure. It got very quiet at the end of our pitch, so finally I just said to him, 'Larry, can we have the order?'

"He told me how thrilled he was that I asked, and how long it had been since anyone he encountered had asked for the order. I was sort of surprised by his reaction, and I just kept quiet. Then he ended the conversation by saying 'I really like that. You've got our business.'"

Great sales performers make believers out of prospects. David Steitz made a believer out of a prospect who didn't believe at first that Characters, Inc., was capable of doing annual reports. He did not prove his point by argument or bragging incessantly about his track record in publishing annual reports.

He brought in the evidence and showed the characteristics of a great actor by getting under the skin of his prospect. He knew what they were thinking and presented his case through their eyes and viewpoints, rather than his own. He says:

"When I was younger, I was much more defensive. I would have tried to verbally prove how wrong they were about us not being able to handle the job. That type of aggressive hostility is the kiss of death for any salesperson. It's a question of not getting emotional and staying focused on what the customer's problem truly is."

PERFORMANCE PRECEPTS TO LIVE BY

Years ago Mary Kay of Mary Kay Cosmetics wrote something in her book that has always stuck with me. She said that every person has an invisible sign around his or her neck that says: "Make me feel important." Through trial and error all the contributors of this book have come to find out that there are many ways to communicate such a message to a prospect. Here are just a few we share with you:

1. **We design a blueprint.** It's a business plan or a proposal that we must have either in writing or inside of our heads. We have to make it our business to walk into our prospect's office with something exciting to say and prove to him or her. We need to know exactly the type of information the prospect desires, and gear our presentation to those needs.

2. **Involve the customer in our performance.** Whenever we can give the customer a feeling of "what it would be like to own our product," we are moving closer to a conversion. At NuSkin, tours run daily for the benefit of the prospective recruit to become involved firsthand. A future distributor visits the Communication Department and listens as hundreds of Brigham Young University students man the phones and com-

puters, staying in touch with over 300,000 distributors world-wide. The head of the Communication Department coordinates meetings, brainstorming sessions, and updates between various regions throughout the world. This system gives the distributor in Michigan instant information about what a Japanese distributor is doing and the size of his downline. Allowing a prospective recruit to become part of the excitement at NuSkin headquarters often causes on-the-spot conversion.

3. We encourage the prospect to ask questions. In the old school sales training days, the motto was keep the prospect in the dark except in those areas that he insists on receiving answers. Today we must go out of our way to get the prospect to tell us the truth. We let the prospect know that we are open to suggestions, can handle constructive criticism and input, and intend to take his or her questions and find solutions to them immediately.

John Marconi climbed the ladder of success by being a proficient problem-solver.

"While everybody else was passing the buck, I went back to the title plant to dig up answers. This is how I created a reputation. I always asked the escrow officers to tell me their problems and ask questions."

Maryles Casto did something similar. Remember her bus tours to the airport with the secretaries? She wanted them asking questions so she could supply them with the ammunition to become indispensable to their bosses.

We are not afraid of confrontation. It's critical that we get all the problems out on the table, because we know high-performance presentation is charged with energy and sometimes high-voltage discussion.

4. We break the silence about the competition. It's no surprise to us that our customers comparison shop.

"I had no trouble asking my customers how my new model compared to the competition. Sometimes it wasn't easy listening to their legitimate gripes or going back to the drawing board to make something right, but customers have great respect for you when you have the courage to ask them who else they are talking to, and why they aren't giving you a crack at it," says John Crean.

Customers feel important when they know that we will do whatever it takes to keep their business.

5. We recommend that the customer talk to our other satisfied customers. Joy Riggs built a 100 percent referral business by suggesting IBM talk to Texaco about her training materials. Evelyn Echols name-dropped all the way to Monaco. With credibility, of course.

Chapter Five Review

- Develop the I-Am-Here-to-Serve-You mind-set.
- Remember today's customer is smart. He or she boldly, but silently tells the salesperson: Know me. Listen to me. Understand me.
- Never forget you are not the only salesperson in the marketplace.
- The service ethic is based on trust.
- Trust creates the relationship.
- Trust reinforced creates more business.
- The customer is impressed by a history of trust-building steps.
- Collaborate.
- Honesty is the basis of collaboration.
- Tell the truth first.
- Truth causes trust to blossom.
- Demonstrate openly your passion for the product.

- Learn ways to extract the truth from the customer. You deserve to know it.
- Accept the feelings, the thoughts, and the logic of your customers.
- Learn how to sell from good actors. They become their characters. You must become your prospects.
- Concentrate on only the customer's agenda, never your own.
- What you sell becomes part of who you are.
- Your passion for the product is always translated outwardly into enthusiasm.
- Without enthusiasm, your presentation will be flat.
- The mediocre salesperson recites boring dialogues.
- The mediocre rarely discover the prospect's true motivation to buy.
- Do not focus on the wrong features, which have no interest to the prospect.
- Do not become a sales exhibitionist.
- Masterful interviewing and listening skills are the tools the pro uses to convert prospects.
- The power behind team selling is the presence of many experts in the room at the time of demonstration.
- Be product rich.
- Give your clients something to help their business.
- How has your prospective client done business in the past?
- Go beyond the original specifications.
- Weave valuable stories into your presentation.
- Stories lead to buying decisions.
- Valuable stories create loyal customers, sales, and good feelings about your industry.
- Physical evidence of quality work speaks for itself.

- Observe your customer's actions.
- Are you monologue selling?
- Take advantage of your mentor relationships.
- Mentors save you time, and teach you the political workings of a prospective company.
- Customers change their minds daily, so continue to stay in contact.
- Allow your customer to talk freely about your competition.
- Invite your prospective customers to talk to your satisfied customers about services rendered.

NEGOTIATING TO UNPARALLELED LEVELS OF CUSTOMER SATISFACTION

*"It's a vision of life as a state of rough harmony rather than war.
You don't live to conquer. You live to care."*

—DAVID DORSEY, THE FORCE

HOW WE negotiate reflects our respect for the customer and
how deeply we care about the life of that relationship. Too
often rising sales stars listen to bad advice about the hard-core
negotiating tactics of peak performers. Peak performers show a
lot of style and grace under pressure which is remembered and
appreciated.

HIGHLY CAPABLE OF WALKING AWAY

"I love to negotiate, but most people hate it. So if you hate to
negotiate, get somebody else to do it for you," says Joanna

"Joey" Tamer, President of Los Angeles–based S.O.S., Inc. Joey is a distribution consultant and expert strategist for new media developers, publishers, distributors, and retailers.

Joey appeared in my life at just the right time. I was moaning to my daughter Beth that I needed to interview a wizard of negotiation. "I'll introduce you to my boss, Joey, Mom," said Beth. Joey turned out to be a wonderful storyteller and teacher.

"When I was about twenty-nine, and was starting my first serious venture capital negotiation for companies, I was taught you never go to the negotiating table unless you are willing to walk away."

Over the last twenty years, practicing this "Zen-like" habit has become effortless for Tamer because "Everything that you say no to leaves open a space for the next thing that comes along that you can say yes to."

Joey backs up every lesson shared with actual experience.

"I just spent $15,000 in attorney's fees negotiating a deal that I walked on in the end. Ate the money. Got nothing for it. Why? Because the deal wasn't win-win. At some point, based on the way negotiations were going, I felt I was beginning to risk my reputation. Nothing is worth that risk."

Tamer says as soon as she walked away, an equivalent offer from another company arrived on her doorstep with no risk to her reputation. Tamer thinks most people feel they have either failed or walked away from an opportunity when they turn something down.

"There is no shortage of opportunity. If you say yes to something, whether it turns out to be good or bad, you still have to say no to the next thing that comes along because you filled up that space."

Joey's detachment in the face of negotiation is the key to her success with her list of clients, which reads like the who's who of the hot nineties companies—Apple, Blockbuster Video, Harper-Collins, and Time-Life, Inc.

"When I negotiate for myself or my clients, I tell them and myself: 'Remember, there is no shortage of business out there.

If this deal doesn't fly, it isn't going to end my career or kill your future business.' "

Keeping this positive attitude is important. When we say no, Tamer advises to be alert because something is going to show up soon to fill the place of what did not work out.

"You may feel awful when something does not work out. But later you will be amazed at how happy you are that it didn't. If it had worked out, this new opportunity that is in front of you never would have presented itself."

We have to believe that what comes along immediately following the lost deal follows a natural sequence of events. There is always opportunity appearing to replace the last opportunity. It's a mind-set, and it takes discipline to think in such a manner.

Joey Tamer said it wasn't easy for her to take $15,000 of her own money and spend it on a deal that she ended up not wanting to do. "If you can't stand the heat, then stay out of the kitchen."

Moral of the story?

"Do not play with the big boys unless you have got the money to lose."

Besides putting our money where our mouths are, Tamer believes in "continuing as well as closing." Continuing means "nonstop courting of future prospects. Then there is never one client who holds the key to your future."

While she travels around the world, she handwrites postcards, makes quick phone calls, and keeps in constant touch with prospective clients. Prospects in the pipeline and money in the bank: It's critical that we have plenty of future prospects waiting in the wings in case our current negotiation efforts do not get off the ground because, says expert negotiator Barry Elms, "The control of the negotiation will lie with the party that is perceived to need the deal the least."

Management Consultant Skip Weitzen investigated the enormous success of Robert Price, the owner/founder of the Price Club, while working on his book *Hypergrowth*. He wrote, "The Price Club established a $250 million cash reserve that fueled its hypergrowth and reduced its costs simultaneously. With its war chest in place, Robert Price canceled his $30 million line of credit, then paid cash for land, buildings, and inventories during the Price Club's expansion."

Dynacom's Allan Gibby knows his company has moved north and matured to success because "We never bought anything around here until we could pay cash for it. And none of us have gotten caught up in lifestyle, prestige, or becoming people we couldn't afford to be."

Our power to negotiate with fairness and good ethics is based on freedom—freedom from debt, freedom from cravings. This philosophy is easy to live by once we are well established in the big time, but how do we make the transformation from inordinately attached to outcomes to peaceful and detached?

We've all been beginner travelers, and we've all felt like we were under the gun. When I was twenty-seven years old, flat broke, and six months pregnant with my fifth child, I was hurting financially. I overcame my own me-directed career, but it wasn't easy and it took time.

We have to ask ourselves common sense questions such as:

Does my desire to feed my family, buy a new car, or take a vacation really have anything to do with my customers?

The pressure we feel comes from conflict about our true intentions. We cannot allow our personal agenda to stand in the way of what we will or will not do for a customer. I needed to learn to let go of self during customer time.

Once we begin to concentrate on the needs of the customer, it feels good. When we find we are so swept away in dialogue with our customer that we no longer have time to worry about how successful we desperately want to become, it is a big relief.

When I feel sorry for myself because I do not know an outcome, I think about a farmer and I feel inspired. The farmer plants the seed then forgets. It's hard not knowing if the harvest will come. We all want a guarantee that our hard work is going to pay off, but we need to forget it and grow up. We must drop our expectations. Those expectations can make us bitter and turn us into greedy negotiators.

We need to stop worrying so much. We worry because we think we *need* to have certain things in order to become successful. I drove a red Volkswagen squareback for the first three years of my career, and I never received one complaint from a customer saying, "I was expecting to be picked up in a stretch limo."

Young salespeople mistakenly get themselves in too much debt because they think that is the only way they can become successful. Both salespeople and sales managers need to quit emphasizing the importance of material goals to motivate sales forces. This practice has burned out talented salespeople and weakened their negotiating power on the way to their own self-destruction.

In David Dorsey's *The Force*, a nonfiction account of "a year's fortunes and misfortunes in selling" at the Cleveland branch of Xerox Corporation, he describes the state of discontent that keeps the corporation, the economy, the nation, and the currency feeding off itself.

"That's what drives everybody toward a more prestigious, slightly more luxurious state of discontent, where everyone sets off to work every morning like a knight on the way to his next battle, his next joust—where everyone lives to win the game or the war."

When we are obsessively hungry, we begin every new relationship with little or no negotiating power. Shakespeare said it best: "He has that lean and hungry look. I trust him not."

There is no need to take the vow of poverty and give away all our material goods. The motivation to maintain an affluent lifestyle is not of itself wrong. Having opportunities to enjoy the fruits of hard work is good and highly motivating. It only becomes a problem when it takes precedent over the needs of the customer.

It is only with the faith of the farmer, the goal of becoming debt free, and the habit of thinking like our customer, that we deserve to come to our customer's negotiating table.

BE PROUD TO SELL YOUR CAUSE

Coach Lou Holtz says, "Once you are fundamentally sound, you must have a sense of cause. It's a sense of purpose that will ignite your negotiating powers and convince your customer."

Lou says we cannot feel embarrassed about selling our cause.

"You better know that you belong there talking and listening to that customer. You are about to make this person's life better, happier, and help him save lots of money in the long run. He does not know all of this yet, but it is your job to show him how this is going to happen."

As our careers unfold, we will have the opportunity to watch our customers become happier or more successful because of the contribution we made in their lives. Experiencing our customer's satisfaction firsthand gives us confidence.

SHOWOFFS ARE TURNOFFS

One of Joey Tamer's clients called her to report he was going back for a third interview with a company, and they were bringing in a former consultant to meet him "to make sure I am not full of hot air."

"The prospective employer brought the consultant in to do a 'reality test' on my client," says Joey.

"He told me during his upcoming interview he was going to tell the employer that their company should be doing electronic distribution because 'It's a great opportunity, and you should be there.' The way he said it smacked of cockiness."

Joey advised him to be tactful, to not show off, but to show "diplomacy with teeth."

Better to say to them, says Joey, "Have you considered electronic distribution? There may be some interesting opportunities if it is investigated."

Her client wanted her to give him a good reason why he should grovel.

"It's not groveling, it is called tact, and tact is very useful when negotiating. You never try to show up the outsider. If your idea is the best idea anybody has ever heard, the consultant will sabotage you because he didn't think of it," advised Tamer.

"You make the idea a suggestion, something that just crossed your mind. Say, I do not really know enough about it but with your expertise on this subject, perhaps you should look into it. Or if you so desire, I can investigate it for you."

Good friend and expert negotiator Somers White agrees. His specialty is handling the negotiation with his client when the client's loan has been called at the bank.

"The client and I have to change the other person's mind."

At such critical times, White says, the client often thinks the best way to renegotiate the loan is to try and impress the bank.

"My clients ask me to go in and negotiate for them, and I highly advise them against such a tactic. The bank doesn't need to think you have some smart accountant or attorney doing the work for you. Instead I try to empower my client, by showing them exactly what to do. The bank wants to see someone with common sense and accountability coming up with some very creative solutions to their problems. Then the bank will work with you."

He says to play down introductions too. If we are acting on behalf of our client, we should not go in to the meeting and allow our client or the host to introduce us as "Mr. Mucky Muck with the Harvard MBA."

"Smart is dumb, and dumb is smart," says Somers.

"It's the Columbo method of doing business whereby you

just ask a few questions and play yourself down. Be more concerned with making the other party a winner and less worried about trying to impress the pants off of all concerned."

LISTEN LIKE A LOVER

To win a tough negotiation we do not need another speech course, but rather more time spent discovering how to effectively listen.

Die-hard caretaker and former teacher Joy Riggs is racking up millions in sales for her company Employee Development Systems, Inc., because she proactively practices listening like a lover. Unlike a tired out lover whose cherished words become boring monologues, she continues to feed her customers lots of respect by being quiet and paying attention.

She landed the tough Sears account after several years of put-offs because she listened so well she even heard unspoken concerns.

"Historically Sears has always designed and delivered their own training courses. Over a period of three years I talked to them about purchasing some of my programs. During certain times they would be interested in this or that, but nothing got off the ground.

"Eventually two key people in the training department became very excited about my interpersonal employee effectiveness course. When it came down to negotiating the sale, however, I heard them each repeat the same concerns to me over and over.

"This was the first off-the-shelf training program Sears ever purchased, and as much as they liked what they saw and heard in my presentation, this was clearly a personal issue for each of the two decision makers.

"I heard one of the decision makers say to me without verbalizing it, 'Look at all I have done. Please see all my past accomplishments. We are not deciding to buy your course because there is something *wrong* with what I have delivered in the past. Please, do you see how valuable I am?' "

By listening closely, Joy discovered he was terribly frightened. She did not win him over by surface flattery, but by truly acknowledging all he had done, and by letting him know that making this decision to buy her course would be just one more outstanding decision he could tally up on the list of his series of wins.

She reassured him continually over a period of months. Whenever a staff member in a big company goes out on a limb and implements a change, there is always great trepidation.

"The other decision maker was the detail person, and she was afraid too—afraid she would not be able to look good as she conducted the nitty gritty of the day-to-day implementation of the new course. She did not have to say a thing. I knew she feared she might lose her job if this was not a smooth transition.

"She desperately needed confidence. I provided support, showed her how to use the leader's guide, and generally tried to enhance her feelings of well-being. I looked for and found the real goodness and wisdom of that man and that woman."

Joy Riggs uncovered some very sensitive issues—discovering how much two people's self-esteem was at stake. There is no powerful sales technique that can replace the presence of someone who really cares and proves it by taking the time to listen. If Joy had gone into the Sears presentation doing all of the talking, she never would have uncovered 80 percent of the information she needed to negotiate properly with her customers.

"You should be careful how much you talk in a negotiation, and you should be careful how many little points you either debate or win," advises Joey Tamer.

"It doesn't matter how we get to what we want, the important thing is that we get there. Let the other guy do all the talking around what makes him uncomfortable about the issues that are being negotiated. Say nothing until he is finished talking."

I learned never to interrupt, because when we do not allow the other party to say what he or she wants to say, while we talk, the customer is only thinking about what he or she wants to say next.

"The fewer words you can win your point with the better," says Joey. This is very difficult to do because we all want to fight every battle, but bottom line, "It's useless to waste this kind of energy, because none of these battles will ultimately matter.

"For example, if your customer is fighting three levels of expense report compensation, when you have won the battle of him paying the expenses, you have to just not worry about it. You cannot go back to fighting over details. This is how most people undo negotiations that took hours to work out," says Joey.

EXHAUSTION

People get exhausted negotiating during long, drawn out meetings, and over the long haul of negotiating for several months. Says Joey, "You are not allowed to get exhausted."

We must do everything in our power not to weaken our position by losing overall energy. This starts with a mind-set, says Lou Holtz:

"Nobody quits unless they think they are not going to be successful. When someone is running in a marathon, as long as he thinks he is going to finish that marathon, he will continue. It is only when he starts thinking he is not going to make it, that he will quit before he completely exhausts himself."

Fatigue stops all positive thought necessary for good negotiations. The will to continue is possessed by the energized.

I ask myself the following questions prior to every negotiation:

1. Did I get eight hours sleep prior to the negotiation?
2. What did I eat?
3. Did I watch my alcohol intake the night before?

I know I have to be in top mental and physical condition. My head must be clear to negotiate successfully. Things go better for me when I walk in to the deal just plain feeling good.

Tamer insists, "If you are exhausted, regroup, wait, and then go back."

A client of Joey's chose the wrong distributor because she got exhausted and said to herself, "The hell with it. Where do I sign?"

Joey said her client went through three-and-a-half months' worth of negotiation and over $10,000 in attorney's fees.

"She was negotiating with the vice president of sales, who was supposed to be the decision maker. It turned out the legal counsel had more power than the vice president of sales. Everything that my client and the vice president agreed upon, the legal counsel refused to write down."

Four months later Joey's client called her in desperation, begging her to take over the negotiations.

"She was totally exhausted, and she wanted me to get her another deal."

The downside is Joey's client had no time to pace herself, because she had held out too long for the wrong reasons. In one week's time Joey got her client the kind of deal the woman wanted from the beginning, but only after a lot of hard work and money was spent in the process.

TRUST THE HANDSHAKE, TRUST THE PAPER

"That doesn't mean you do the deal on a handshake," says Joey. But it is a reminder that if the handshake is no good, what good is the paper? A friend of mine with a Harvard MBA learned in school that lawyers are hired to get their clients out of other lawyer's contracts. Bottom line is if you cannot trust the paper, the handshake is the only thing that is worth trusting. This means the whole negotiation is only valid where a true relationship, trust, even friendship exists."

Author of *Phone Power* George Walther says, "When George Burns has an idea for a book, he tells his personal manager about it, who in turn calls his agent, who in turn calls the publisher."

Walther points out that all these people trust one another and have an ongoing relationship between them. Most of the negotiating has taken place over the phone, and contracts are merely delivered by courier after the fact.

"When Harold Weisbrod, Chairman of the largest jewelry manufacturing company on the west coast, wants to acquire another jewelry company, he mounts a relationship by developing a campaign using a series of phone calls spaced out over months," says Walther.

Dr. Sharon D'Orsie claims it is "the strategic alliance and partnership that makes most of our negotiations go smoothly. Because the problems that we solve are technically very difficult, we end up working collaboratively with our clients to solve a problem. Our negotiation style is friendly."

Shirley Pepys's reputation in the juvenile products industry is one of caregiver. In the high-tech, impersonal society of today, "It is more important than ever to genuinely care. My negotiations with Toys R Us came after the fact. I became close with their buyer in Germany. We admired one another. It is so much easier to negotiate with the trust factor in place. In business you simply must spend the time getting to know each other."

For instance, Pepys found it difficult in her early negotiations with Sears because she did not have a relationship with their buyers, but she had the license to the Paddington Bear, the signature character who was replacing Winnie the Pooh.

"In some ways we were forced upon each other because I had the license. An outsider thinks the hot item to have is the license, but the license with no relationship established is meaningless."

Carolee Friedlander says, "Credibility is established in a trusting relationship. You are not just negotiating a sale. You are continually going back to the negotiating table with the same people over a period of a lifetime."

She's been doing business successfully with the same people at Bloomingdale's for the past twenty years. "It's a cliché, but the people you meet on the way up, you are going to see again on the way down. How can anyone separate negotiating from relationship building?"

The Force details the loyal, long-time client relationship Xerox copier salesman Larry Tyler had with John O'Neill, whose mother was dying of cancer. In the middle of negotiations Tyler could have easily upgraded O'Neill to a more expensive copier in the state of mind O'Neill was in — exhausted, rushed, worried about getting back to his mother's bedside, and ready to sign anything to get the order completed.

But Tyler genuinely cares more about his customer's pocketbook than his own personal agenda. In this particular instance Tyler needed to bump up the O'Neill sale in order to "make trip" (an expression used at Xerox to describe the annual trip to Palm Springs for the top performers who make their quota).

Author David Dorsey wrote, "O'Neill asked, 'Listen, do people do reduction and enlargement a lot in my kind of business?' "

This was the key question that could have negotiated a bigger commission check into Tyler's pocket.

Tyler responded with, "No, you don't really need that feature."

Carolee, Tyler, Pepys, and the whole team repeatedly prove that Dorsey's theory—"that a salesman can make a living by serving other people with compassion and intelligence and genuine friendship"—is not just theory but common practice up north.

PINPOINT MOTIVATION

Pro negotiator and IDEA founder Peter Davis knows from past experience with some of his mega sports and athletic wear sponsors that discovering what is *motivating* the person on the other side of the table is critical.

"Once I start seeing things from my client's viewpoint, then I determine how to create a win-win negotiation."

One company may be motivated by a desire to improve their image in the woman's athletic market. Another company is motivated by the pressures of a new product launch and market exposure. It may not be kosher to vocalize the client's true motivation during negotiations. The client knows we know. The only thing that is necessary is to make what they need available.

Peter Davis discovered "If you have what the customer is asking for, then the customer begins to sell themselves to you. You put it in front of them, and you listen to their reactions and concerns."

"It's not always money," says entrepreneur and paint supply manufacturer Robert Davidson of Surface Protection Industries, Inc., in L.A.

"I made a bid on some real estate once and was flatly turned down by the owner. Out of the blue six months later the same owner called me.

"He offered to sell his building to us for less money than we offered, but said there was only one stipulation—we must close the deal in thirty days. Time was his hot button."

Innovative salesman turned entrepreneur Jim Gagan created a buyer's membership club "because I heard people wishing out loud for 'an uncle who could get what they wanted for them wholesale.'"

His sales team negotiates new members into the club by focusing on consumer's motivation:

"Suppose that you had many uncles who owned dozens of businesses. One was in the furniture business, another in home appliances, another in sporting goods, and others in many more. Imagine that each one of these uncles agreed to sell you practically anything you wanted to buy at his cost."

Pinpointing people's motivation has paid off big for United Consumer Clubs, whose sales exceed $100 million and link over 500 manufacturers to 500,000 consumers.

"Speed without sacrificing quality and budget was the motivator behind my shot at the big time with Ocean Pacific (OP)," says Allan Gibby of the time he got his big call from the vice president of OP.

Previously Dynacom had done two corporate videos for OP, but was yet to get an opportunity to shoot the world renowned OP national surf contest.

"There was a legal falling out with the company that was going to do the work that was to be aired on KABC. The VP at OP called two weeks before the OP Pro to tell me their TV deal fell through and he was wondering how fast we could come through. I convinced him the job would be first class and completed on deadline."

Gibby hit OP's hot button. "But the pressure was on. We knew we had to make good on our promises. Once we proved ourselves, our future credibility at the negotiating table dramatically improved."

BE BRAVE THROUGH THE TENSION

Joey Tamer knows how to break the tension during tough negotiations:

1. Stay Put, In Spite of Yourself.

"I am in a deal with an Israeli company and a distributor. Both sides are my clients. [This is not legal for lawyers, but it is for consultants.] At one point the clients came to a total breakdown of negotiations. The distributor was very angry because his offer was completely rejected in the middle of the meeting.

"There was enormous tension and silence in the room. The first notion would be to walk out. But you cannot do that."

Joey was the negotiator in the middle and it was critical that she stay silent. "Everyone will tell you that it matters who gives in first. It doesn't matter which side opens their mouth, as long as it is not the negotiator. It only matters that the parties come to a consensus."

As she predicted, she stayed silent and her clients resolved the problem.

2. Use Humor for Levity.

Two other clients of Tamer's were trying to work out a merger. In the meeting, "One won't say what he wants; the other won't say what he is offering."

Four hours later none of the parties were as yet willing to put the deal on the table.

"The one that needs to be acquired does not know what to ask for, and the offerer does not want to make the offer because he knows if he shows his hand he will lose points."

Finally the man put a framework of an offer on the table, and the tension and silence build even more. At that point Joey realized that this offer was probably as good as Leo, the seller, was going to get. The silence was thick.

"Leo, you are a pregnant girl in a small town, and you have got to marry somebody," blurted Joey.

Tamer says that both parties laughed so hard that they forgot they were upset.

"A few minutes later we all went to a much more friendly round of negotiation."

AVOID THE HARD AND FAST POSITION

Somers White advises against playing the tough guy in your negotiations.

"One of my clients purchased a company from a man and all the negotiations were very successful. But two weeks after the deal was completed, the seller ran into the buyer and mentioned that the acquisition did not include the name of the company.

"Can you imagine if you bought Coca-Cola and then after the fact you were told you could not use the name? The seller told the buyer that the attorneys had dropped off the final papers and no one had spotted that the name was not included. Up until then the sale had been a smooth one.

"The buyer panicked and asked the seller what was going to happen. The seller said, 'Why don't you buy me lunch, and I'll consider lunch the payment for the name?' "

Because the buyer left feeling as if he got so much more than he bargained for, he will respect and spread good rumors about that seller for the rest of his life.

Entrepreneur Robert Davis calls that "leaving some of the marbles on the table. Let the other guy be amazed. He should walk away thinking he got a lot more marbles than he thought he was going to get."

Somers White shares this: "There was a piece of commercial property that a salesperson was negotiating. The numbers broke down like this: 10 percent of the money was going to the salesperson, 45 percent was going to his company (commercial broker/developer), and 45 percent was going to the large insurance company that was funding the project.

"After the deal was written up, the commercial broker, who

was supposed to get 45, rips up the papers and says, a good deal. We are going to give you, Mr. Insurance C 50 percent and reduce our company's share to 40 percent.

White asks, "Do you think when that same commercial b ker came back to the insurance company three weeks later to negotiate another deal, he had any trouble getting his financing for the next project?"

Skeptics may call all these goodwill stories a form of manipulation. They can call it what they want, but even if the insurance company knew the commercial broker was schmoozing them, they loved it. It is important to note that when this commercial broker/developer got in trouble during the hard money times of the early nineties, this developer was the one the banks did not sink. Why? Because their style was always "Leave a few marbles on the table for our clients."

George Walther recommends asking a negotiating partner the following question after the deal is done:

"What little extra thing can I do to make this transaction even better for you?"

He says most of the time the customer will reply with "Nothing," but will always remember that we are willing to go the extra mile and do whatever work is called for over and above the call of duty.

When David Steitz was a younger salesman, he learned the hard way never to take a hard and fast position.

"Most often I will give in to the client rather than hold my ground, even when I know I am right. This was not the case when I was a young salesman. At the time I was working on an annual report project, and the designer who I was working with had made a mistake inside the book and it cost him several thousand dollars. So he came back to us—his suppliers— and admitted he made a terrible mistake, and would we absorb the cost of his mistake as a favor?"

David says he had only been around for a few years, and because he was young, stubborn, and inflexible, he took a very hard and fast position.

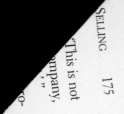

"This is not ...mpany,
...-

y should I have to absorb the cost of
? *That is just not fair.*'"

man and gave him only a fraction of
thought I was doing a really great
ore negotiator?"

elf on not bending. "I would say
knows what me giving into this guy
would have led to.'

"Well, I'll tell you what it would have led to—me doing several hundred thousands of dollars more business with this person and his firm."

Five hundred dollars and his principles were the issues. "For that I cost our company several thousands of dollars in lost business."

It took several years to gain that business back. "I sat down and talked to this man years later. I told him that was about the dumbest thing I had ever done. Yes, I think there are times when we have to stand for our principles, and be aware of what the consequences are. But when I was young, I was not a good listener.

"If I had been less of a talker, less of a my-way-or-the-highway kind of guy, I could have felt more empathy for a man who admitted quite candidly that he had made a cost analysis mistake—a mistake that we all are capable of making. This wasn't about honoring my principles, it was about massaging my ego and satisfying my need to be right. Some folks spend their entire life preferring to be right, rather than happy."

Steitz learned that the pros do not talk at or preach to a customer. "If I had really listened, I could have heard him with a more empathetic heart, and together we could have devised a more creative solution to his problem."

George Walther suggests we think to ourselves: "What is right? What is going to get everyone closer to a desirable goal? Is it really worth holding back a piece of the pie? Is it our prin-

ciples or some irrelevant personal pet peeve that we are defending? There is a big difference and it could cost us a lifetime customer."

The Four-Way Test

In the area of limits of liability and indemnification, Sharon
D'Orsie says many customers do not want to negotiate.

"They just want me to be in charge of the universe, in case
anything goes wrong. That is not okay. So I make it clear we
will be responsible for a maximum of $100,000 worth of dam-
ages, in case something goes wrong."

D'Orsie uses the Rotary International four-way test as her
negotiating guideline when things get sticky.

The test uses four questions to determine how a negotiation
is going:

1. Is it the truth?
2. Is it fair to all concerned?
3. Will it build goodwill and better friendships?
4. Will it be beneficial to all concerned?

"In my industry we have hard hats and safety shoes. What
happens if we are working in a plant and the place blows up?
Most of our clients want to write the contract stating we are responsible for the blowup or whatever else happens just because we happened to be working in the plant. On the other
hand, the client wants to be responsible for nothing.

"I set up clear boundaries and detail parameters. I write out
what mistakes I will be responsible for and what mistakes I will
not take responsibility for. These are the type of issues that
must be spelled out to avoid later misunderstandings."

An Objection Is Not a Rejection

Joy Riggs's client's objections empower her. With the Sears account she discovered that the decision makers initially objected to issues that were not the things the parties were really worried about. Joy listened *under* the content of their words and found out each was worried about losing face or compromising his or her position in some manner. Besides listening carefully, she compassionately repeated verbatim what each party revealed to her. She desired a deeper understanding of each person's viewpoint.

An objection is like a fever. When the body becomes infected with virus, the symptom is a high temperature. The fever is an indication of a deeper problem. The doctor prescribes aspirin to bring down the temperature, but he or she also begins to ask a lot of questions. What did you drink? Were you around anyone who was sick? Then the doctor does a complete physical and runs tests to find out exactly what is ailing the patient, and what a lasting treatment might be.

Ninety percent of the solution to a problem is understanding what the problem is. This is why the doctor is more interested in getting to the source of the sickness than in merely treating the fever. Somers White consistently uses this medical model to negotiate more business.

There were eight agencies vying for a bank's business. One of the competing advertising agencies hired Somers to help them figure out how to get the business. When Somers helped them land the account, no one could understand how the agency that came out of nowhere won the business.

"I investigated why the previous agency had lost the bank's business," says Somers. "In essence I confronted all previous problems/objections head-on because I knew that if I could pinpoint objections, I could pinpoint what types of issues would be motivating the bank to make a decision on this go around."

White found out that the last ad agency had lost the business because of their sloppy methods of billing, poor record keeping, and shaky financial history.

"All of the competing presentations centered around how creative they were. We showed them how we handle billing, and gave a history of our financial health and sound credibility with local TV and radio stations, etc."

Somers flattened the toughest objections, objections that were completely unknown to the competition, by confronting and offering solutions to previous problems.

We must never attack the objection. It is not a personal rejection against us. We need to step back and think for a moment. We must listen to the emotion of the objection. Is the emotion fear because one or both parties are afraid to negotiate?

Or guilt because the party is insisting on winning a point he or she does not necessarily believe in?

Or anxiety? Because the prospect likes our proposal but wants to make some changes without offending us, or risking having us walk away?

Joey Tamer negotiated a chapter in a book with Apple Computer for over three hours by telephone.

"They started out by sounding panicked and saying, 'We have to restructure this whole thing again.' " Joey was used to the other party's initial panic reaction. She knew that the party really wanted her work, but some changes would have to be made, and the other side did not know how to say it directly.

Heida Thurlow is convinced objections are merely necessary dance steps in the negotiating of any deal.

"It's a coming together, then going apart again. It helps me to keep this image of a dance in my mind during negotiations. Then I do not get too emotionally involved, and I also tell myself there is a rhythm and a pattern of movement connected with the negotiations I must go through this with the customer. Sometimes we get close and sometimes we must move apart."

"I realized a long time ago that objections are only questions in disguise," says Evelyn Echols. "I eavesdrop every chance I get on my customers."

Evelyn walks through her travel schools once every ten days and tells her students that if they have any problems she will be glad to chat with them.

"If people come in with a complaint and it is valid, there is not much peace in our organization until we get it straightened out.

"Sometimes I run up against tough people who demand a full refund on their tuition at our travel school. No questions asked, I offer to pay the full refund. The ironic thing about it is that they never take it. From that day on that person is a different student. Sometimes all people are negotiating for is attention. This is their way of saying 'Give me my money's worth.' "

Giving individuals the opportunity to present a problem or a complaint to us takes the sting out of the objection. The objection flattens, loses its power, and everybody is ready to get down to business.

Jim Rhode answers all complaint calls, and "It blows the customer away when the boss calls them directly. They tell me their problem wasn't really that bad, and they appreciate the call. I always end up giving the store away, but when I hang up I know that I have negotiated a customer for life."

Taking objections personally ricochets in many negative directions. We start to feel anxiety or fear and become defensive by blaming the company, suppliers, or anyone, in order to save our customer relationship. Other times, out of fear, we ignore the objection and change the subject abruptly. This is very irritating to a customer. We have to learn on the way up to stop this pattern of behavior.

To uncover hidden objections that still may be lingering during the negotiating phase, ask fervent questions. Author Linda Richardson says, "Questions offer you the opportunity to fix things during the course of the negotiations."

We can behave very confrontationally without offending. Here are some of my favorite negotiating questions:

What outcome would please you most?

Are the necessary resources in place to make the decision at this time?

If I personally promise you to accomplish each item listed, will you give us a shot at your business?

If you do not invest in this component, will it be sorely missed over time?

Without it, will your growth and productivity be inhibited?

Up to this point in our discussions have you found anything that is really bothering you that you need to talk about or tell me to change?

STAY FOCUSED ON THE ISSUES

We work our way through each objection by staying focused. Heida Thurlow says, "Sometimes one of the negotiating partners may try to sidetrack you or mess up your rhythm."

Heida takes a pad of Post-it notes with her while negotiating.

"Nothing too large or intimidating. It's just meant to be a little reminder note for me."

On each page she writes down one issue that must be confronted and resolved during the negotiation. Usually there are around five issues on the pad.

"When I start feeling like myself or somebody else is off the beat, I look down and remind myself where we need to go, and this keeps me focused. Only when I feel satisfied that we have discussed these issues thoroughly do I cross them off my list."

"Take the issue of flying first class versus coach class across the country," says Joey Tamer. "If the client begins arguing money, do not get sidetracked into his or her thinking."

Here's what Joey suggests we say:

"Look, you are paying me $2,500 a day to arrive on the other side of the country and be smart. Would you prefer to pay $2,500 a day for me to be stupid?

"I will be stupid if I fly all day uncomfortably, do not rest, and am expected to be bright at 4 A.M.—my biological time—for the presentation."

She advises we stay on the issue, which is not money, but energy.

Sharon D'Orsie says if it sounds like money is the biggest issue in the final stages of negotiation, that is the time to break the problem down into systematic steps and focus clearly on each issue.

"I know my downside limits when I go and negotiate with a customer. The three issues I hear that my customer cares about most are money, liability, and limits on liability and indemnification."

If her customer responds to her presentation positively but admits he or she wants to spend less money, or if the customer says the amount of services Sharon is suggesting does not match the budget that is available, that is when Sharon gets very organized and systematic.

She negotiates that point by saying, "I propose we do the project in steps, meaning initially we cut down the scope of services."

She is suggesting to the customer that instead of "doing the air quality monitoring in seventeen factories this year, why don't we do it in three?"

Somers White says, "I take my negotiations step by step. I teach my client to make a conscious effort not to worry about the next part of the negotiation."

He says focusing on one single point at a time goes back to the earlier lesson about being a good listener. Like Thurlow, White takes notes to help him stay focused and he asks permission from the client to do so.

He tells the client, "When I finish taking notes I will give you a copy of the notes."

This is not common practice, and he believes it improves the trust factor between him and the other negotiating partner.

Most negotiators are taking notes to "trick the other guy," says White, "but I am doing it in order to not take advantage of the client. Everything is documented. There is no going back to the client later on and misquoting, or arguing over who said what."

Often the item that gets the most attention during negotiation—price—is not really the important issue after all. For example, a couple may be negotiating a great price on a home across from the railroad tracks, but the couple have two small children. So is the price really worth the worry and grief they are going to have after they move into a house that is in an unsafe neighborhood for their children?

Price is sometimes not what it appears to be. The lowest price often bears the highest cost. A young couple borrows $5,000 from the family to make a down payment on a house. They pay interest and eventually pay the loan back, but they get to hear about the loan for the rest of their lives.

Finding out the real issues is an important step in high-level negotiations.

CREATING A SENSE OF URGENCY

How can we be patient and create urgency at the same time? By not using urgency as a ploy. A real sense of urgency builds from the moment of first contact with the prospect, and it culminates powerfully at the time of final negotiations, prior to the closing decision.

We cannot isolate the negotiating sequence and say, "Okay, now it is time to push and shove and box this guy in. Now is the time to try the good guy/bad guy routine, and then if that does not work I'll jump to the choke-hold routine."

A sense of urgency is set by deadlines. Whoever sets the deadline has the power.

"I was having dinner with a client at a hotel in Johannesburg, South Africa," says Somers White, "and I asked him as we sat down to dinner if he had to be finished with our dinner meeting at any special time."

The man told Somers that "Tonight is my anniversary. So I do not want to be too late."

"As soon as he said that, I knew I had just made the deal with the man on my terms."

On the other hand don't assume deadlines cannot be changed. A legitimate way to avoid that is by deferring to a higher power, which takes us off the hook and keeps the doors of opportunity open.

If the door is about to close, we can tell the customer we want to go back to the purchasing department, our sales manager, or our partner and see if someone can sharpen a pencil one more time.

For example, if I ask for a price on one hundred audiocassette albums and then tell the salesperson that his figure is over my budget, he may defer to a higher power and then end up tripling my order.

"Danielle, if you increase your order to three hundred sets, I can give you the price you have budgeted. I understand you do not want to pay for or take delivery on those three hundred albums today. Would it make sense for me to deliver and charge you for the one hundred albums and then over the next ninety days you can take delivery on the rest of the order?"

If we use this type of approach to negotiate an order, we must be sure we understand who our customer is. To one customer this suggestion may come across as very inappropriate. "Sure, I got my price, but now I am stuck with three hundred audio albums."

Other customers would appreciate the option because they know they will probably sell the first hundred easily, and would be reordering more very soon, so why not get the price break?

We need to remember our deal does not have to be struck at the moment. If things are not moving effectively, there are many reasons we may want to defer to a higher power. Where there is hope, a small ray of light peeking through the doorway of negotiation, we should practice patience. In six months we may be glad we did.

STYLES OF NEGOTIATING

We do our homework by acquiring an understanding of the negotiating styles of those we do business with regularly.

"Some countries have a very orderly way of negotiating, and to violate that order in any way is offensive to that negotiator. Other people are offended when the negotiation is unduly rushed," says Somers White.

"When Averell Harriman went to the Paris Peace Conference, he rented a suite at the George V Hotel in Paris for two weeks, and the Chinese, whom he was negotiating with, took a lease on a villa for two years."

White says this is a reminder that in different societies people want to move either slower or faster, and it is up to the visiting negotiator to know the preference.

The first day of the Paris Peace Conference, the Chinese requested that the rectangular table be changed to a round one before negotiations started.

"They understood that some furnishings communicate a 'them against us mood,' and that is not beneficial to anyone."

In some countries we must go through a third person who is responsible for the negotiation. Say someone's daughter wants to go to work in the company where her mother works. She will then go to see a third party who will see about the daughter getting the job. The daughter gets the job, but it turns out she is not doing a good job.

That same third party who talked to the mother about seeing to it that her daughter be considered for the job, is now in charge of talking to the daughter about the poor quality of her work.

"Third parties add more pressure to all negotiations," says Somers.

White says they have an expression in the Orient: "Favors granted, and obligations recognized."

The lesson? Sometimes we are so busy thinking about what we want in a relationship or negotiation, that we forget the obligation, the accountability factor, that goes along with the privilege.

In some countries, the little things are the big things when negotiating.

"In Java, a young man of a lower station in life fell in love with a woman from a higher station. The young man's mother came to call on the mother of the girl," says Somers White.

"The girl's mother welcomed her, and asked the boy's mother if she would like some tea. When the tea was presented, a sliced banana came on the tray with the tea."

The two mothers talked very pleasantly, but they never discussed the marriage of their two children.

"In Java fruit is never served with tea. So the message was 'The banana doesn't go with the tea, and your son doesn't go with my daughter.' "

White travels to other countries frequently to negotiate and he says,

"The alertness to subtleties in some societies determines the success or failure of negotiations. In America 75 percent of the emphasis in the negotiations is placed on the deal, and 25 percent is put on the relationship. In most of the other countries the opposite is true."

Chapter Six Review

- Respect the customer.
- Show grace under pressure.
- Be willing to walk away from the negotiating table.
- Nothing is more important than your reputation.
- Walking away does not mean failure.
- There is no shortage of opportunity.
- Stay detached.
- Keep a positive attitude at all stages of negotiation.
- Opportunities present themselves immediately following a lost deal.
- Don't play with the big boys unless you have the money to lose.
- Continue to court customers at all phases of negotiation.
- One client never holds the key to your future.
- Negotiating power comes from ethics and freedom from debt.
- Your sense of cause empowers the negotiations.
- You are about to improve your customer's life forever.
- Earning your customer's confidence gives you negotiating power.
- Be tactful.
- Listen like a lover.
- Keep your customer's self-esteem in tact.
- Say little and listen much.
- Beware of your own exhaustion diminishing your negotiating powers.
- Nobody quits when they presume they will be successful.

- If you are exhausted, stop negotiating temporarily.
- Trust the handshake, trust the contract.
- What is motivating your negotiating partner?
- Let the customer sell him or herself to you.
- Money is not the only negotiating issue. Time may be more important than dollars.
- Be brave through the tension.
- Use humor for levity.
- Avoid taking a hard and fast position.
- Leave some marbles on the table.
- Amaze your negotiating partner.
- Find out from the customer what you can do to sweeten the deal even more.
- Give in to the client, even though you feel you are right.
- Do not preach to a customer.
- Remember an objection is not a rejection.
- Pinpoint issues and problems.
- Listen to the emotion of the objection.
- Do not ignore true objections or try to change the subject.
- Focus on one single issue at a time.
- Establish a sense of urgency to set deadlines.
- Deadlines can be changed.
- Third parties add more pressure to the negotiations.
- Put the emphasis on the relationship, not the deal.

CHAPTER SEVEN

TRUST, COMMITMENTS, AND ASSUMING THE SALE

"Blessed are those who can give without remembering and take without forgetting."

—ELIZABETH BIBESCO

"GOOD SALESPEOPLE get a bad rap because closing the sale is the most overrated part of the sales process. I never close. I assume they are going to buy from the very beginning and then the sale just happens," says Joe Gandolfo.

He is right. My own first sale just happened. While driving my red Volkswagen squareback, nobody was more amazed than me when my backseat prospects tapped me on the shoulder and said, "We want it."

"You want what?" I said.

"We want to buy it."

"Don't you want to think it over?"

Don't laugh. I needed a week cloistered in the bathroom to figure out how to fill out the paperwork.

Twenty-three years later I am here to report why my first sale came together:

1. *I Was Properly Prepared.*

There is a big difference between prepared and *properly* prepared. Properly prepared means being exact and precise. Plain old prepared is too general. I was forced to learn about precision during my first interview with the prospects. They warned me up front that I would have only one shot with them.

If I delivered the goods, I would make a sale. If I didn't come up with something completely different from what they had already been shown, they were going to go back to their other salesperson and settle for less than what they really wanted.

I had to do some serious researching during the three days prior to our meeting. I knew my inventory, merged it with my customer's needs, and created a sale.

2. *I Was Duly Amazed.*

When my buyers said, "We want it," I was amazed. They found my amazement refreshing.

"Without any expectations, you went right to work for us," they said.

The travel queen Maryles Casto puts it another way:

"Stay in awe."

She calls "staying in awe" her closing attitude, the attitude she has kept since she was brand new in sales.

"I never expected the Intel travel account to follow me when I left my last employer to go open my own travel business. My old boss made me promise not to contact clients or to attempt to take their business over to my new company.

"I kept that promise, but one month after I left, the vice president of Intel was upset because he wasn't getting good service from my replacement so he demanded to know where he could find me.

"Yes, I had earned his business, but I was truly in awe when he called, and I won over the account."

Sound like a contradiction? We prepare, believing we are going to close the sale, but we don't count on it. But then if we do close it, we are amazed.

3. I Assumed, But I Didn't Presume.

Joe Gandolfo says, "It happens because everybody now has faith in my solution. It's all based on trust, pure and simple. Either the trust is automatic from the first moment you meet or it isn't. You can forget about closing if the first meeting gets off to a bad start and certain trust issues never get resolved. Nobody can go back and meet someone again. If it's right, it's right.

"When someone says 'I want to think about it,' they are really saying 'I do not trust you.' "

It's a salesperson's basic goodness that establishes trust.

"If you close hard, you are compensating. You missed something along the way. For example, a man walks into the room, and before he opens his mouth, the salesperson tries to sell him a Cadillac. The guy wants to buy a radiator belt.

"It's pure stupidity. Where does that salesperson get off thinking he knows what the man wants before the man has even opened his mouth?"

SELLING EXCITEMENT AND THE WINNER'S MIND-SET

The salespeople in this book learned to sell through intuition and imitation. We watched salespeople we admired, who made the sale the way we wanted to do it, and then we imitated them. Eventually we moved beyond our models and carved out our own unique way of creating the sale.

For instance, I learned how to generate excitement by watching Monty Hall. When I was twenty-six years old I appeared on his game show "Let's Make a Deal." I was speechless when he approached me on the trading floor and announced on national television:

"One of these three keys fits into what is behind that curtain. Pick a key, my dear."

I picked key number three. Then the curtain opened and a brand-new chocolate-brown British Leland sports car miraculously appeared in the middle of the stage. Then Monty grabbed my hand, and together we raced down the ramp to see if I had just won myself a car. Monty had generated even more excitement by grabbing the key out of my hand and running ahead to see for himself if the key fit.

Monty loved to drive the audience crazy by putting keys in doors upside down and yelling out, "I . . . I . . . I don't think it fits . . . No, it doesn't fit . . . or does it . . . wait . . . wait . . ."

In selling we call that "the old take-away."

The audience was screaming at a fever pitch.

"Pick number one. No, it's number two. Don't be stupid, lady, it's number three."

By the time Monty yelled, "It fits," I was in a state of true ecstasy, as he announced, "You, Danielle Kennedy, are the proud owner of a new 1970 Stag Sportscar."

With Monty every deal was a celebration. He was possessed with a winner's mind-set: the you-have-the-power-to-beat-all-the-odds mind-set. He infected people with a contagious feeling that something wonderful was about to fly out of nowhere and if you paid attention you could catch it. Being in his presence filled me with a belief that anything was possible. Monty got me hooked on the selling high—a spine-tingling moment in the sales process when all the invisible forces come together and the customer says, "Yes."

BELIEVABILITY

Insurance superstar Lin Lam has believability.

"The winner's mind-set comes from an intense belief in the product. I hypnotize people, and my will and the strength of my commitment cannot be broken.

"Mediocre salespeople do not have that kind of conviction. They will try to sell anything if it makes them money, but they give up easily when a close isn't apparent. I never give up, because I am convinced nothing could take the place of my product in my customer's life.

"On the other hand, I won't sell it if I don't believe in it. We used to have a worker's compensation program with an insurance company that was not doing well. The company wanted to sit down and renegotiate the contract with me. I looked at the files and noticed attorneys were suing everyone, and the program was not a good business booking. I didn't believe in their program, so I cancelled the presentation."

Legendary stockbroker Jack Sullivan learned the importance of believability and commitment from his own father, who invested on Wall Street.

"My father went out of his way to buy the products of the companies he invested in. He bought shares in companies like Colgate and then their products, such as toothpaste, etc. Not that it made a meaningful difference to Colgate, but it did to him. He wanted to commit to the products of the companies he invested in. I have built my business on a similar belief system. No client of mine ever invests in a stock that I haven't invested in myself. I don't think of myself as a salesperson or a closer. I am a partner with every one of my customers and every one of my companies. If I don't buy, they don't buy.

"In addition to co-investing with my clients, I also co-invest with the owners of the companies I buy. I look for quality owner-operated, publicly held companies that have fallen below the radar screen on Wall Street for one reason or another. I start the process by calling up the chairperson, who in these companies is likely to be the founder as well as the single largest shareholder, thereby getting a whole lot of information and perspective with one call.

"He or she is inevitably pleased to hear from someone interested in their stock. There is a founder's pride, combined with a frustration with Wall Street because the Street hasn't recognized the value of their creation.

"My eventual goal is to raise the company's level of visibility in order that the inherent values be realized. After satisfying myself as to the quality of the situation and the viability of the investment, I personally buy stock in the company and invest my selected group's funds. My risk reward is always the most substantial, as it should be. I am there with my clients 100 percent of the time."

When Jack approaches the companies, he asks, "Would you consider coming to San Francisco and giving us a presentation?"

He says he must have access to the chairman (founder, largest shareholder) or he won't get involved. Since there is very little published information on these companies, access is mandatory.

"Once we meet for the presentation, I look for reassurance that management is working for shareholders. In the meeting we learn about the presenting company, its competitors, and their prospects. Then I make a decision whether to invest.

"Potential investors should ask any broker if he or she owns the stock being recommended. All too often the answer is no, and that is completely unsatisfactory. Why would anyone want to buy a stock that someone recommends but doesn't invest in himself? That is merely passing on an idea without any commitment. Everything we do here is based on belief and commitment. It means putting your money where your mouth is and, only then, asking others to do the same.

"I don't have a closing philosophy, just a hard-work philosophy. One happens to close as a result of doing a lot of preliminary hard work. The results I get are strictly a by-product of what I do."

Companies like Fidelity and J. P. Morgan value Jack's beliefs too. They pay him for his advice and research.

Angel Martinez says yesterday's consumer used to put up with salespeople who didn't believe in their product.

"You can't get away with that in today's marketplace because there is too much quality competition. I do not believe in surface-level selling. You sell what you believe in, like selling part of yourself."

There is nothing Rich Luisi believes in more than Electrolux cleaning systems. His sales record proves he turned his beliefs and enthusiasm into millions of dollars of earned commissions.

"I've sold over 10,500 Electrolux cleaning systems in the last twenty-four years. My excitement comes from ownership. When I demonstrate one, my customer knows I am an Electrolux owner, not just another vacuum cleaner salesman.

"My parents owned the system when I was growing up. There is a built-in enthusiasm with me. It's very real, and my customers know I am not faking it. How can anyone get enthused about something they do not believe in?"

Luisi always comes up with new ways to use his Electrolux. Once he mixed a solution of laundry detergent, poured it into the rug shampooer, and removed oil stains from his garage floor.

"When you own what you sell, you discover what the system can do. I bring an authenticity to the demonstration because I experiment, and then I use my experiments on my customers to make sales.

"Because I am an owner, I am an excellent Electrolux salesman. There are too many salespeople selling products they do not use themselves. Why would you want to buy a Mercedes Benz from a salesperson who drives a Lexus? If someone is not

110 percent sold on what he is selling, the customer will read it loud and clear."

I insisted my friend and the author of over thirty business books Robert Shook be one of the great sales teachers of this book. He is a best-selling author for two reasons: He is an outstanding writer, and he possesses seven figure sales skills. Other talented writers could use those sales skills.

Bob says, "If I didn't believe passionately in what I write, I would not have gotten published in the past, or the present or the future."

In spite of his proven credibility, writing autobiographies of such business greats as IBM's Buck Rogers and Mary Kay, as well as his own best-selling books such as *Hardball Selling*, Shook still counts on his extraordinary sales skills to keep him published.

"My newest book, *The Greatest Sales Stories Ever Told* almost didn't get published, until I closed the deal myself. The book was a collection of sales stories with lessons highlighted at the end of every story. My agent loved the book, but he struck out with twelve different publishing houses because, typically, editors do not like salespeople or the books they write.

"Here's how I sold it myself. First I asked myself, What do I have to do to sell this book? I called an editor friend of mine and told him a little bit about the book. He liked what he heard and told me to send him a copy of the manuscript.

"I called him back a few days after he received it, and he told me he was high on it, but everything was done by consensus and the other editors didn't like it. In passing he mentioned he was going to a sales conference in California the next day. I asked him to do me a favor and take the proposal with him on the trip, and let a few of the salespeople scan it.

"Then I asked him to strike up conversations with people on the airplane and ask them for their opinions.

"I made him promise me he would do exactly what I asked,

and then report back to me when he returned home. If he received even one negative response from any of those people, I'd forget about the whole project.

"He was on the phone with me five minutes after he returned to his office. 'You were right. Everybody loved it.' We struck the deal that week."

Tony Parinello sold his way into the Hewlett Packard sales force on sheer belief.

"When I made a decision to leave corporate management and go into sales, there was only one company I wanted to work for—Hewlett Packard (HP). I had used their computers earlier in my career as a lab technician and respected the quality.

"I interviewed with the sales manager and told him I wanted to sell their stuff. He said I was well qualified except I did not have a four-year degree. This was a strict requirement at HP.

"I begged him to give me a chance. I told him I loved their computers, knew how to use them well, and knew what it took to sell them. I'd rather be on the HP sales team than anywhere else in the world.

"The man said his hands were tied, and he didn't have the power to hire me, but he told me who his boss was. He appreciated my tenacity, but warned me that the higher up I went, the more I would get the same negative answer. They only hire college grads.

"I booked an appointment with his boss. During the interview his boss said to me, 'Boy, you really do know our products. There is no doubt about that. What college did you go to?'

"I told him I never went to college, and he told me he could not hire me. Then I told him I had heard that from the other guy during the last interview, but he just had to give me a chance, and I knew he would never regret it. He kept saying 'I can't hire you,' and I kept saying 'I believe in it. Give me a chance.'

"I probably wore him down, but I liked HP's equipment more than anyone else's stuff. Somehow my belief got across, because finally he said, 'I am going to hire you on a handshake. If you fail one test in your training program (they had an extensive testing and training program), you must quit because I cannot fire you once I hire you and you enter the program.'"

On a handshake Tony Parinello was hired.

"I was the only guy ever hired on the sales force without a college degree. And that is probably true until this day. I never failed one test. I got my field assignment, and the first year I was named 'The Rookie of the Year' and a member of the Million Dollar Club. My years there continued to be very successful."

Tony's convictions, and his willingness to tell the truth and stretch himself, form his style of assuming the sale.

"Because I do not have a college degree, I have always felt I had to prove beyond a shadow of a doubt that I was highly capable of doing a great job. This is how I convince people to hire me, buy my products and services. It's how I open opportunities, and opening opportunities is what I consider the closing process."

TUNING INTO THE PROCESS

Closing is not part of the sales process, it *is* the process.

Tony Parinello says,

"Too many salespeople charge forward in the sales process because they want to hurry up and close something. When they hurry ahead, they do not realize that the customer is back at the starting line, nowhere near ready to make the size of decision the salesperson may be asking for.

"Selling is a series of mini conversions. Taking little baby steps forward with some customers, and giant leaps forward with other customers. If we are further ahead than our customers, it is the result of not specifically asking the right questions and listening to exactly what the customer is saying," says Tony.

"Questions like 'I am willing to give you a thorough tour of our plant. At the end of that tour would you be willing to tell me your true feelings about what you saw during that tour?

"'Will you be prepared to tell me if you see a future between my company and your company at the end of that tour?' "

Joe Gandolfo piggybacks on Tony's advice:

"Selling does not mean presuming. Selling is listening. How do we know what the customer wants? We know because selling is asking. 'How can I help you? What color? What price range?' It's a simple process—just give people what they want. If we sell people what they *want*, then we are going to get the opportunity to go back and sell them what they *need* the second time because they thought we were so brilliant to let them buy what they wanted the first time."

Gandolfo backs up everything he says with an experience from his glorious sales history.

"Years ago this world famous man calls me up and wants to buy a policy to cover the $16 million he borrowed from the bank. One day he passed out at work, and a kid that worked for him gave him artificial resuscitation and saved his life. I had just sold that kid a $10,000 insurance policy. In passing, this man asked the boy if he knew of a good insurance man. Of course he did.

"The man invited me down on his yacht. I just listened and then wrote up the policy. Since then he has referred me to a ton of his multimillionaire friends and he has bought millions more from me too. Why? Because I shut up and gave him what he wanted the first time. I just listened and followed instructions."

Rich Luisi now manages over twenty-five hundred other Electrolux salespeople and he passed on to me what his legendary sales career has taught him about the art of assuming the sale:

"Everything in the sales process is a form of closing. It's a seamless presentation whereby qualifying is closing, demonstration is closing. In the process we are creating enough need and building enough value that the customer *wants* the product. There is no need to apply pressure. Because we qualify to close, and because we demonstrate to close, there is no set time where the buyer says to him or herself, 'I am being closed.' The entire presentation is a closing opportunity."

Rich says if the customer feels he or she is being closed, the salesperson is most likely more interested in his or her own needs than in the needs of the customer.

"There are those types of salespeople, the ones that give the entire profession a bad name. They are both pushy and awkward. It's like being chauffeured around by a guy who keeps pumping his foot on and off the brake. You can't wait until you get out of the car because his driving is making you sick to your stomach."

The pro is not obnoxious, but has self-respect, knowing he or she has the God-given right to find out up front how serious the buyer really is about buying.

Rich says, "When a genuine pro and a legitimate prospect come together, the sale starts when the qualifying starts, and the prospect accepts the proposition to buy from the beginning. Either you are going to find out you are dealing with a serious buyer, or you are not. Get to work and ask at least fifteen to forty questions. If the prospect says yes enough times, he or she will eventually say yes to the sale.

"If I could show you how I could make this carpeting look like new . . ."

Luisi starts all of his qualifying questions off with the word "if."

A series of "yes's" leads Rich to the final close. "No one is going to keep saying yes until the last minute. I know very early in the demonstration if the prospect intends to buy my product."

Brenda Burke from Pecos Learning says, "I know instinctively right away, within minutes, whether I have a serious prospect in front of me. I don't prejudge, but I can see through the baloney fast."

Strategic planner Joey Tamer says, "I assume they are going to buy from the beginning or I wouldn't be there. But when the time for a decision comes, I contradict myself. It's my most successful method of drawing decisions out of people. It's called 'The Ask and Give Them Permission to Wait Until They Are Ready' Method:

" 'I want your business. I know I can help you get it right the first time, saving you millions in mistakes later. But you should not begin until you are ready.'

"This is the best closing statement I know, because it's true. I don't care if they have the money and were dazzled by my presentation. If they are not ready to listen, I don't want to work with them, at least not yet. It's like throwing their money out the window.

"So when I ask if they are ready, I am really asking if they are ready to listen, learn, and change. Customers find this challenging because they know I am not about money, and I am willing to wait. Waiting never bothers me.

"When I get resistance, I tell them to call me when they are ready. But I add, 'Currently we are booking six to eight weeks out, so keep that in mind when you call to book my time.'

"I don't say this as a pressure tactic. It's just true. Although it really makes the customer think twice about letting me walk away. People call up and get mad because I talked to them a week ago and now I can't drop everything to go work with them."

Tony Parinello's "What is your personal yardstick" closing question, which he formulated with Mr. Dean, has evolved into an even stronger question because of his strong personal beliefs in his own capabilities.

"I go directly to company presidents and say, 'Let me ask you the one question you want your salespeople asking presidents of companies that they call on:

" 'If I can measure up to your business criteria, which you just shared with me, could you see yourself becoming one of my customers now, or by the end of the quarter, or year?' "

No longer afraid to start at the top, Brenda Burke uses similar language:

" 'What do you need most in your organization right now? I am here to help you get it.' That's my magic question. When the CEO knows my intentions and I know his or her expectations, eventually I will be able to assume the sale."

THE MONEY ISSUE

When money becomes the roadblock, Joey Tamer doesn't fight it.

"When people say, 'Gee, that is a lot of money,' I say, 'Yes, it is. It's the same amount of money attorneys are paid, and they are some of the highest paid people in the world. I'm paid what they are paid, and for that you will get the same degree of excellence you would get from a first-rate attorney.

" 'Remember, I am a strategic planner—the person who shows you how to get it right the first time. For this amount of money you get it right the first time, and then you are going to be free to make your millions without being encumbered.' "

Sometimes the roadblock appears to be money but it's really the customer's perception of what they are getting for the money.

"I have a friend who had to change her product's packaging from 'product positioning' to 'market analysis' or 'competitive analysis,' " says Joey.

"I told her that no one would buy 'product positioning' because the vice president or the president does not want an out-sider positioning their product. He thinks he knows all about that facet of the marketing. So my friend needed to give him product positioning, because he really doesn't know as much as she does about the research, but instead she calls what she is offering 'market analysis and competitive analysis,' and leaves him the information to make his own conclusions from, which are her conclusions, but it appears he figured it out himself."

The message is that when we can't sell something the client doesn't want to pay for but has to have, we must position our services or package our product to appear to be the thing the client does want to pay for.

For example, I know that when someone calls me to do a speech on customer service, they are going to go through the wall if I send them information on sales skills or I talk sales skills on the phone to them. Customer service people are not fond of the word "selling."

But the ironic thing is a person with strong customer service skills has the same skills as a strong salesperson. The customer service rep and the salesperson both need to go the extra mile, follow up fastidiously, and turn complaints or objections into opportunities. But with certain companies I cannot package my programs using the word "selling." They call it customer service, and I am not about to argue with them.

The price is intricately wrapped up in the packaging. They do not have a budget for someone who is arguing with the meeting planner over the phone about how selling skills are really customer service skills. But they do have the budget if the speaker calls herself a customer service expert and proposes a customer service program with no mention of sales.

There is no deception here. A good salesperson must be an expert at customer service. If we don't know about customer service, than who does? If a company wants me to come in and train their personnel on customer service and none of them have ever sold in the field, they need to hear what I found out in the field about customer service.

Beware of answering money questions, such as "What is the range of your services, and the price range of those services?"

"Dangerous question," says Joey Tamer. "Don't back yourself into a corner with your answer. Instead of shooting off figures, better to say, 'What is it that you need, and then I will get back to you immediately and tell you what we can do about it.'"

DON'T CONFUSE THE SALE

"You have to assume they do not need anything, and that they are calling you on the phone ready to hire you. Once I tried to divert a sale by telling a man who called in that he should meet me in Boston to discuss my services. He never asked for a meeting with me in Boston, but I felt compelled to offer one. He was ready to hire me on the spot," says Tamer.

References and endorsement letters are great if they are asked for, but if the customer doesn't ask for anything except a quote, or the opportunity to do business with us, we delay the sale by offering unnecessary steps.

Throughout the sales process we must never lose sight of what continues to motivate the customer. Any benefits of our product which have nothing to do with the customer's personal desire to buy must never be mentioned.

I learned to quit making noise—wasting time dispensing irrelevant information—and to start concentrating on adapting to my customer's style of doing business. My first buyers only required that I hand them the pen so we could get on with the deal. Other customers took months to decide, requesting a continual repetition of previous information for clarification purposes.

ADAPTABILITY

Ken Rohl believes the number one reason most average salespeople don't graduate to the big time is their inability to adapt
to the customer's style of doing business. He must adapt to not
only different personality styles, but different countries' cul-
tures.

He learned during one critical closing moment the importance of adaptation. A year after he opened his U.S. offices and
formed a partnership with European-based KWC, the senior
management in Europe went through a complete turnover.
The board of directors terminated the chairman of the board
and the chairman's son.

These were Ken's partners, and they were being replaced
by professional management consultants. His relationship
was in jeopardy too. His challenge was to save his job, his
company, and a potentially prosperous future alliance with
KWC.

"As soon as I got the news, I jumped on a plane to Zurich.
When I arrived, my son told me that our former partner, who
was being terminated, had made a proposal to the board to
take over the U.S. distribution. Suddenly my partner was my
competitor.

"I knew it would be a challenging presentation, but I had
spent twenty-five years preparing for such a moment. I had a
strong foundation with dealers across the country. I directed
my thoughts to those who would be attending the meeting. I
evaluated what they would be most concerned about, and
then I decided how to center everything I said around their
concerns.

"I brought a map of the United States with me. I felt it
would be the best graphic I could use to explain to the Swiss
people the advantages of partnering with me. I tacked the map
on the wall, and circled major markets of the U.S. as I explained my distribution strategies.

"I advised my colleagues to focus on what I considered high-potential, high-performance market areas. This also allowed me to differentiate between those markets that were ready to be developed in the first stage and those that would be coming along later."

He talked about how the east coast, especially the New York Metro market, was very high potential. It was already conditioned to European products and would be the perfect place to start their European distribution.

"With previous positions in other companies, I had serviced that area and knew excellent distributors in New York. These people were friends of mine who had already been contacted and would agree to distribute the product.

"I moved on to Boston and pointed out similar benefits. Then I explained that we would not go to the southeastern part of the United States initially. They were not prone to European products. It was more of a retirement community, and they did not have the disposable income the west coast had.

"Then I jumped across to California, choosing that as my third highest potential market. I also requested to make California the KWC headquarters. The pool of 10 million affluent people, and the contacts I had there, made it a logical choice."

Ken knew that KWC's board and new executive team were very logical and street smart, and would be most impressed with an intimate knowledge of the various U.S. markets. As his presentation moved along, he sensed they were liking what they heard.

"The room got much friendlier. I started out not knowing what I was up against, but as I progressed I felt more and more confident. I was now ready to let them know I was confident in my position, and I decided to call for a decision.

"I did so by using confrontational language, but with a tone of deep respect for both the other people's time and my own.

"I turned to the CEO and said, 'You know, I feel a little intimidated. You are sitting there with an attorney and giving me the impression that an agreement I have with the former owners may be in jeopardy.

"I, on the other hand, have come on my own with what I feel is a very authentic presentation on the advantages that you will have with my company and with my partnering with KWC in the U.S.

"I tried to make it clear to you in this last hour that there is a strategy that will work and I know how to implement it. I am going to leave this room and go out into the reception room and wait thirty minutes. If you choose to go forward with me, please come out and invite me in and let's get on with the agreement. If you choose not to, I will understand and say good luck to you."

Within fifteen minutes the CEO invited Ken back in and advised him that he was the exclusive distributor of KWC in the U.S.

"When I walked into that meeting, I did not know exactly how I was going to close, but it didn't matter because I was prepared. A closing strategy can never take the place of preparation.

"If I had gone in there without that map, I do not know if the outcome would have been the same. There was a big language problem. The majority spoke Swiss and French. They would not have been able to understand a business discussion without the map."

It was more than Ken's map that wrapped up that sale. He did his homework, adapted his appeal to his clients' needs and concerns, and asked for a commitment after he gave his clients enough closing points to convince them how right it would be to keep him on the team. The timing of the closing question determined his credibility with the customer equally as much as his demonstration of knowledge.

"Americans who want to do business globally must adapt to subtle differences. We all do business for different reasons. It's important to be able to take direction from our customers across the globe," says Ken.

"You have to learn to speak the customer's language," says Tony Parinello. "Especially in the computer business, where the techies can confuse a customer right out of a sale. I was out on a very complicated demonstration when I was still with Hewlett Packard. The president of the company was sitting in the meeting along with myself and my systems engineer, and my manager was standing next to me.

"We are about thirty minutes into the demonstration, my systems man was talking computerese and his fingers were flying across the keyboard, and I began to notice my customer's facial expressions changing. I could tell he was completely lost. His whole body was in a slumped posture.

"When you take someone like the president of a company, who has that much ego, power, and authority, and you challenge him with a knowledge base that he is unfamiliar with, you are in trouble.

"I panicked as I saw my customer shrinking. So when the systems engineer paused and took a deep breath before diving into the next part of his spiel, I interrupted and said to the president, 'Do you have any questions, Vito, that I can answer for you?'

"With this lost look on his face, he asked me probably the only question this man could think of: 'So how much memory does this machine have?'

"The question was totally unrelated to the demo, but it was probably the only question he felt safe asking. I looked at him and said, 'Vito, this machine will never forget anything you tell it.' "

Tony said that after he made that comment, his systems engineer and his manager gave him looks that could kill.

"They expected me to say that it has four megabytes of main memory, which is expandable to eight, but if you put our fast four eight transformer, etc."

But Tony didn't say that. He adapted himself to his customer, who needed to understand the whole mess in layman's language.

"The president laughed and said, 'You know, Tony, finally something I understand.' The systems man then dived in and did the rest of the presentation. The president went home and my manager called me into his office and told me never to give a smart-aleck answer like that to a customer again.

"He lectured me about working for a technologically driven company and advised me to answer such questions in a more professional manner.

"About eight months later the president bought the system. I took the $240,000 purchase order into my manager's office, slid it across his desk, and said 'I just sold the machine that will never forget.' "

Tony's smart-aleck remark saved the deal. Adaptability means many things in the sales process. When a salesperson tries to impress a high authority in a company during a sales presentation with language or demonstrations that are over the client's head, the salesperson is actually threatening that executive's power base. It's sales prevention. It's a form of sales malpractice/exhibitionism, and it all stems from a lack of adaptability to those that we serve.

THE DEATH OF A SALESPERSON

Rich Luisi describes closing as being "pleasantly persistent, to the point where the customer knows that everything you are saying is true, and he or she cannot say no. This is very different from being aggressive.

"Aggressive salespeople concentrate on making a sale. Persistent professionals concentrate on building a business. The customer can smell the difference. There is never a reason to apply pressure when need and value have been established."

Pressure closers are pests and cause the death of their own sales. I watched one die a few years ago on my own doorstep. I was told by my attorney to purchase some disability insurance as soon as possible. I trust my attorney implicitly, so when he offered to contact a friend of his who sold this type of insurance, I agreed wholeheartedly, once again proving how powerful a third-party endorsement is.

My schedule is very tight so the man called me on the phone, introduced himself, asked me some questions, and told me I would need a medical exam. He would handle the scheduling and other details with my secretary. He was very accommodating, but I never actually met him until the day he delivered the policy.

When he brought it over, we stood in my entry hall and chatted briefly. I thanked him for the service and then he did something way out of line—he attempted to close another sale without determining if I had a need, or making an effort to demonstrate any type of benefits, handle objections, or negotiate. Just when I thought he was getting ready to leave, he looked at me and said,

"By the way, I talked to your attorney and told him I went ahead and drew up a $1 million life insurance policy for you. The premium on it is $1,000 a month, but you will have it paid off in twelve years."

I was speechless. Of course he took that as a positive sign to continue.

"Now, if this doesn't work, I also have a term policy in my briefcase for the same amount, but it's only $190 a month. However, this rate keeps escalating and you will have to pay higher premiums on it the older you get. I would definitely go with the whole life policy, if I were you."

I wanted to say, "You aren't me, and it is obvious you do not know what it is like to think like me. I have all the insurance I want, thank you, and I have no intention of buying more, especially after purchasing some very expensive disability insurance."

Instead I bit my tongue and said, "I'll talk to my husband about it." I suppose I could have educated him on his foolishness but he was so matter-of-fact about it, I was convinced he would not understand the error of his ways. He called the next day and wanted to know what my husband thought. I told him we were not interested.

There are lots of ways to kill the sale, but none is as deadly as prematurely asking the customer for a commitment which is undeserved. We all must satisfy the customer's needs as well as his or her hunger for information, and proof of product value, *before* proceeding to commitment.

If we do our homework with care, closing will be a logical and natural next step. If we haven't done our homework, we are just like the student who shows up at the final exam completely unprepared but attempts to sit through the test. He or she takes stabs at the multiple choice questions using the "When in doubt pick letter C" method.

SPOTLIGHT THE BIGGEST NEED

It's only the desensitized salesperson who runs up against all kinds of roadblocks while trying to close the sale. He or she is so preoccupied with getting the check or demanding a signature that the customer becomes defiant and not about to move an inch toward finalizing the sale.

Closing the sale is not a struggle. It can be the easiest part of the process if we focus in on what is truly important to the customer. Rich Luisi had no trouble doing that with one customer.

"One time I was doing a home presentation to a customer who was allergic to bees. Whenever the woman saw a bee she panicked. A bee came in the room about one hour into my demonstration and she went nuts. I sucked up the bee with the vacuum cleaner. That was all I needed to do to sell the machine."

He had another customer who was paranoid about insects.

"I put the crevice tool on the vacuum cleaner, sucked up some crumbs along her kitchen counter, and wiped the tool clean with my white test cloth. When I opened up the test cloth about twenty-five ants appeared on it. That alone was enough to make her buy.

"You never know what is going to turn your customer on to buy your product. That is why you need a complete demonstration. Mediocre salespeople do not deliver a thorough demonstration. With Electrolux we are delivering a cleaning system. To me that means we must demonstrate cleaning every floor surface and other surfaces in that customer's home.

"That customer must see how well it cleans carpets, stairs, couches, and mattresses. Most people do not know that the human body sheds one layer of skin every month and that most of it is lying in the carpet. This is what causes odors, and dust mites."

A rug shampooer and floor polisher is part of the cleaning system. Rich has spent hours with a prospect spit-shining every inch of her home.

"Because every customer's needs are different, I have to spend the time taking them through all the benefits because I never know until I am in the middle of the demonstration what is considered by my customer to be the most important feature of my product. Once I know, I focus in on that particular benefit." One woman bought because she was impressed by the way the attachments reached under the bed.

When a customer spotlights complaints, we shouldn't run, but use the complaint as another opportunity to close the sale.

"My most rewarding closing moments came when I was able to take a customer's complaint and turn it into a sale. The ironic thing about this type of situation is the complaints were not product related, but salesperson related. For example, the product was sold too fast, without the proper installation, or education of the customer. She did not have answers to questions that she needed."

Luisi says not giving the customer any vacuum cleaner bags, or not letting the customer know where he or she can purchase the bags, or not responding to a customer's phone call regarding such requests, are the typical errors made by mediocre salespeople.

"The performer loves details. He supplies the customer with more bags than can be used in a year. He leaves lists of authorized dealers and toll-free numbers. He responds in a New York minute to the customer's every call and wish."

Ken Rohl's next closing story reinforces Luisi's belief: "I can turn any problem into an opportunity. One of my favorite closing moments was with the manufacturer of Italian shower heads," he says, "because all the cards were put on the table immediately.

"We met in Paris at another trade show, and he spoke no English and I spoke no Italian. The export manager for KWC was a woman who was fluent in five languages. I approached her and told her I wanted to strike a deal with this Italian manufacturer and I was concerned because we had no common language.

"She agreed to be the interpreter. The Italian wasted no time spotlighting his greatest concerns.

" 'Does Mr. Rohl pay his bills?' he asked the interpreter.

" 'Does he have strong national distribution?'

"Once I provided the evidence to go along with his two questions, I counter-closed him.

" 'Do you deliver reliably?'

"I asked that because there was concern that some Italian companies were not as conscientious as they should be about deliveries. Then I asked if I would have an exclusive relationship with his company on their products."

Rohl and the Italian found a perfect fit of values and continue to do a lot of business. Ken knows that his customer is going to be specific about what he wants at the beginning of each new deal. Ken in turn centers his entire closing presentation on nothing but the stated issue.

At Danielle Kennedy Productions, I sell hundreds of video training systems a year and almost all the prospective video owners bring up the same concern.

"I love your system but how can I get my staff to use it?"

I then spend most of my time discussing how to implement the program and keep the staff motivated to continue to use it. In this case it would be stupid to spend too much time talking about how the whole curriculum will increase the sales teams' productivity. A workbook on that subject has been developed giving specific guidelines to follow.

CONVINCING CUSTOMERS THEY NEED YOU

"My first sale was a Chinese man who owned the Gaslight Motel in southern California," says insurance legend Lin Lam.

"He could not read English and was impressed that I did. He insisted I read the entire policy word for word to him. Understand I didn't read English that well myself, but I convinced him I read better than he did and I understood what the policy meant. Twelve years later he is still my customer. My first year I sold over one million insurance premiums because I convinced many Chinese people they needed me, based on my primary reading skills.

"Then I got so busy I began hiring and training other sales agents who could go out and handle all my business. Sometimes when they finished training they wanted to leave me and open their own company. I have watched other top producers get very angry with agents who wanted to go off on their own. Why get angry? I saw their restlessness as another opportunity.

"I sold them on the idea that they needed me. If they sold their product and I placed it with an insurance company, then it was a good deal for them. They didn't have to worry if their knowledge was lacking or they couldn't get a company contract.

"I convinced the other salespeople that if we stayed together we would have more power than any of us would have operating independently.

"We wrote $30 million in premiums. All of this started in one split second when I thought to myself, I can either fight them, or lead them."

And this little dynamo does.

"I am five-foot-two and I still stumble with my English, but that was not going to stop me from landing the Islay account."

Islay owns half of the apartment complexes in Santa Barbara. Lam says the owners and controller tested her will.

"Islay sold one small property to a Chinese man who gave me the lead. So I cold-called the controller and said, 'I think I can offer you better insurance. Can I come up and see you?'

"I drove up to Santa Barbara and there were three partners in the meeting. They found me amusing. You know. Chinese woman, five-two, one hundred pounds, who thinks she can handle this giant business account. I kept saying, 'Give me a chance. I will do a good job.'

"They just looked at me and smiled. Then they asked one another if they should give me a try. They both laughed and said 'sure' and sent me to the controller. I was shaking and in a way they were having fun with me, but I didn't care.

"Then the controller treated me like dirt. He didn't want to change insurance brokers. He was set in his ways. The controller didn't care that the owners had sent me to see him. He did not believe I could handle such a big account. But I kept following up with phone calls to remind him I wanted their business.

"Plus I didn't mind winning on my knees. You have to stay humble. Let's face it, his boss told him to see me and allow me to give him a quote. He couldn't say no, and I could have played into that. Instead I mentioned what a good job the owners said he was doing.

"It took a while but I finally landed the account. They became one of my best accounts. A few years later one of the owners said to me, 'I used to watch you park your car in the vacant lot across the street from my office. Then this little itty bitty girl would get out of that car, with a big briefcase, walking with her head held high as if she was head of some large brokerage house. I admired you from day one.'

Lin never thought of herself as small potatoes.

"I told them there wasn't a big brokerage house in the world that could give them the kind of service they would get from me.

"When you are coming up, you are convincing because you want their business, and you have to be dramatic about it. You have to put your life and your survival on the line. I told my first banker I would go hungry, give him my last bowl of rice, to pay back my debt. He believed me because I was sincere. To prove how sincere I was I went out and bought a life insurance policy and made the bank the beneficiary.

"After you reach a certain level of credibility, closing is easy. Now the tables have turned, though. Recently I needed a loan and two banks were trying to sell me on doing business with them."

Edie Fraser feels that convincing people that they need her really means "Motivating another person to pay for my service. This is a big order, especially when your goods are expensive. If they are not sold on me, they will have no motivation to buy from me."

"Never forget that you are convincing people that you can

help them get what they want better than anyone else can. Bottom line is you are selling you," says Coach Lou Holtz.

When Do You Stop Asking?

There is a lot written in this book about persistence and the never-say-die attitude. Does that mean it is never appropriate to let go of a customer? Do legends ever give up?

When I was a novice, I bought into the philosophy that it was always my fault when I didn't close the sale. In the seventies the accepted thinking of other salespeople and management was Why didn't you get the check? It's your fault. You did not close hard enough.

Salespeople were taught 150 different strategies and closes. I noticed that many salespeople who seemed very good at "getting the check" were highly intimidating. Yes, the customer gave in, but that same customer canceled the sale as soon as he or she was released from the intimidator's clutches.

My closing experiences were mostly positive, and there was never a need for arm twisting. I often reassured the customer that what he or she was about to do would pay off in the long run, but it was never a tug-of-war between myself and the customer. On those occasions when the close started to move in that direction, I learned that enforcement and intimidation made a tense situation even more uncomfortable than it already was.

So what did I do when by all rights the customer should have been signing on the dotted line, but for some reason, out of the blue, in the eleventh hour he or she began to resist? I found out I did not have a closing problem, but a truth problem. Most of the time something had come up that the prospect was afraid to tell me. The prospect bought from a competitor or had changed his or her mind. Instead of facing the music by confessing the truth, in order to take both of us out of misery, the prospect became very critical of my product.

For a while I played the game, trying to defend every new objection. These were objections that never came up earlier in the relationship. That should have given me my first clue that I was not dealing with a standard closing problem. Finally, one day, out of complete exhaustion, I threw my hands up and these words came out of my mouth. I call this dialogue the "Stop Closing Dialogue":

"Let's pause a moment and figure out what seems to be the problem. First, let me say that my desire to serve you has always been much stronger than my desire to sell you.

"You should want to buy this more than I want to sell it to you. Up until now I thought you did. But suddenly I find myself defending all the reasons I thought you wanted to buy. I do not like being put in that position.

"If you decide at this point not to proceed with the sale, it will not be the end of my career, nor will it offend me. But what would really be upsetting is if you do not reveal what is bothering you about our entire negotiation at this stage of our relationship. So there is only one thing that is important right now: What is on your mind that you need to share with me?"

After I said it, I shut up. I knew it was critical that no words be spoken by me after asking such a direct question. We must give them a chance to confess and then make it okay once they tell us they no longer want to buy what we have to sell. I have bitten my tongue until it bleeds, but said nothing. We must be gentlemen and ladies about the whole thing. It's really the same principle I used with my children when they were growing up: "You will never get in trouble for telling me the truth. Only lies count against you."

By the time they were in high school it wasn't always easy hearing what they had to confess, but it kept the doors open through the tough times, and now that all but one is an adult, I am happy to report I birthed my best friends. When we give someone the permission to be unconditional with us, we are opening the opportunity to build a wonderful relationship.

In sales the same rule applies. Let them confess and they will love us forever. Two years later a stranger will come through our door and tell us he or she wants to buy our product. The stranger has been referred to us by Mr. Heartbreaker, who put us through the ringer twenty-four months ago. Now we have to call old Mr. Heartbreaker and say thank you for the new business. We must never burn bridges.

"The customer is looking to you for honesty. You, in turn, are looking to the customer for honesty," says Rich Luisi.

"A telltale sign that your sale is not going the way you want it to go is that the objections are all different.

"For example, the customer says to me 'I can't afford it.' And she says this to me say twenty or thirty times throughout the demonstration. Eventually I will probably believe her. But if she tells me, 'I can't afford it. I have to talk to my husband. I do not have time. I have to pick up my kids.' In other words if she gives twenty different objections, I know I'm not getting anywhere with her."

Luisi reminded me that if a salesperson believes in the law of averages, then knowing when to bail out becomes a plus.

"Expect the 'no's.' Get them out of the way, and then go to work."

Tom Hopkins puts it even more clearly: "Each no brings you that much closer to the next yes."

Chapter Seven Review

- Assume the sale. Don't presume the sale.
- Closing is based on trust.
- "I want to think it over" means "I still do not trust you."

- A salesperson's basic goodness establishes trust.
- If you are closing too hard, you are compensating for your lack of knowledge about the product or the customer.
- You do not know what the customer wants until he or she tells you.
- Develop your intuition, and use it to guide you in closing.
- You imitate salespeople who sell the way you like to be sold.
- Belief is the most important invisible force behind asking for a closing decision.
- Own what you sell.
- To sell is to close; to close is to sell.
- Slow down.
- Selling is a series of mini conversions.
- Selling is not presuming. Selling is listening and asking.
- Follow your customer's instructions.
- Strive for seamless presentations, where qualifying is closing and demonstrating is closing.
- Sell to serve.
- No need to apply pressure.
- All presentations are closing opportunities.
- Do not make your customer feel he or she is being trapped into making a decision.
- The sale starts when the first question is asked.
- Questions uncover the truth about the seriousness of your buyer.
- The customer who says yes enough times buys your product.
- Never prejudge.
- Assume they are going to buy from the onset.
- Use endorsements to close the sale.

- Stay focused on buyer motivation.
- Do not speak unnecessarily.
- Adapt to the customer's style of doing business.
- Adapt to the customer's culture and environment.
- Be pleasantly persistent.
- Prematurely asking for a commitment can kill or delay the sale.
- Closing the sale should not be a struggle.
- Customer complaints can present more opportunities to close the sale.
- Peak performers love details.
- Closing takes seconds and is very easy.
- Speak from the heart.
- Does the customer want to buy your product more than you want to sell it?
- Each no brings you closer to a yes.